KING DAVID

MASTER Class

Soyinka Sonuga

COVENANT PUBLISHING

King David Master Class
Soyinka Sonuga

Unless otherwise stated, all scripture quotations are taken from the Holy Bible, New King James Version (NKJV). Other versions cited are NIV, KJV, GNB, God's Word and NLT.

ISBN 978-1-907734-07-6
First Edition
First Printing February 2016

No part of this publication may be reproduced, distorted or transmitted in any form or by any means, including photocopying, recording or other electronic or mechanical methods, without the prior written permission of the author, or except in the case of brief quotations embodied in critical reviews and certain other non-commercial uses permitted by copyright law.

For permission requests, write to the publisher, addressed "Attention: Permission Coordinator" at the email address below

Covenant Publishing
samadewunmi@btinternet.com

Covenant Publishing is part of New Covenant Church
Charity Registered in England & Wales number 1004343
Registered Address: 506-510 Old Kent Road. LONDON SE1 5BA

Copyright © February 2016, Soyinka Sonuga
All rights reserved

Cover Design by Covenant Publishing Team

Published by Covenant Publishing
Printed in the United Kingdom

Acknowledgement

First of all my deep appreciation goes to God almighty for the inspiration to write these few pages; what started as just jottings from my daily bible study snowballed into a concise literary work.

My appreciation also goes to my darling wife Julie Soyinka-Sonuga, you have been a dedicated pillar of support and encouragement all through the years. You also knew how to gently nudge me into developing my passion for writing. Thanks also to my son David Oluwasemilore Sonuga for pushing me on with your desire to see the finished work.

I appreciate Bro. Dimeji Awoyemi and Sokunle Sonuga for reading through the early drafts and offering their criticisms and suggestions. Thanks also to Ayodeji Sonuga for reading through the manuscript and the inspiring feedback. I am very grateful for the invaluable contribution of Simbo Olorunfemi in proof reading and editing the manuscript.

Finally, I acknowledge the encouragement and support of Pastor Sayo Akintola, Pastor Sam O. Adewunmi and Sotayo Sonuga.

Foreword

This is a valuable resource for all leaders and students of leadership. It brings out biblical, time-tested principles of leadership that is applicable in the various settings of home, ministry and secular, from someone with some experience in these areas. The principles also apply in government.

It is written in simple and clear English that everyone can understand. I will therefore commend its readership to all in positions of leadership and those aspiring to such positions."

Obafemi Omisade
National Overseer, New Covenant Church, UK

Preface

This is a book about the expressions of leadership and consequential lessons based on the acts of one of the greatest personalities ever in the bible. There is no other person in the bible apart from The Lord Jesus that the account of his life is that well documented.

I have been a keen student and critic of leadership over the years having had the good fortune of observing and studying leaders over the course of my professional career and ministerial work. I have worked and risen through the ranks in marketing management at some leading consumer goods companies; over a 14 years career in Nigeria starting at Cadbury Schweppes, then British American Tobacco and finally The Coca-Cola Company. On relocation to the UK and over an 8 year period, I have had the privilege of being a marketing practitioner at United Biscuits, Nestle UK, PZ Cussons International and a brief stint at Fastjet Plc. I have also been involved in Church ministries as a volunteer in different roles for over 25 years.

I did not set out to write a book; I was about the course of my regular bible reading when the Holy Spirit started to draw my attention to specific things in the life of David. The more I read, the more fascinated I became that such truths have been right there in the open yet hidden. The leadership lessons will be very familiar to students of leadership, but what makes this unique is the fact that they were expressed in the course of life of a single individual. What academics and leadership speakers teach as theories and ideals had been actively demonstrated thousands of years before hand by an individual who did not have the good fortune of such formal grooming.

This book is biblically based but the lessons are generally applicable to all. I have followed a pattern of looking through the stages of life and acts of David as expressed in the scriptures and then drawing out the relevant leadership lessons. David was not always right in his various actions and reactions (there is no such thing as a perfect human being), but his flaws in some of the episodes discussed in this book still demonstrates some leadership characteristics. I have tried to avoid the theoretical trap of using the often mentioned textbook principles and then using episodes in the life of David to back them up; rather I am showing that David exemplified leadership greatness over the course of his everyday life chapter by chapter. Using artistic license, I deviated from the chronological order in the last few chapters in order to make the last chapter a sort of summary and call to action. It is a book intended for any individual who aspires to becoming a great and effective leader rather than just being any other leader.

Table of Content

Acknowledgment	iii
Foreword	v
Preface	vii
Prologue - The Man David	13
1. Be discerning	27
2. Be honourable	37
3. Have a sense of self-worth	43
4. Demand competency	53
5. Be a loyalist	59
6. Be decisive	65
7. Be compassionate	71
8. Be team minded	81
9. Build alliances	85
10. Justice for impropriety	89
11. Place value on your assets	95
12. Do not be a title only in name	101
13. Be consistent and principled	107
14. Be unassuming	113
15. Do not be presumptuous	117
16. Learn from previous mistakes	121
17. Give honour	127
18. Identify with others	133
19. Get the right support structure	139
20. Manage setbacks	145
21. Plan for posterity	153
22. Fulfil your role	161

PROLOGUE

The Man David

On the night Jesus was to be arrested, as he talked to the disciples, he made reference to a prophecy in Matthew 26:31,

> *"Then Jesus said to them, "All of you will be made to stumble because of Me this night, for it is written: 'I will strike the Shepherd, and the sheep of the flock will be scattered.'"*

This prophetic statement highlights some interesting facts worthy of note:

1. The flock of sheep is lost without the shepherd

2. The easiest way to attack the flock is to smite the shepherd
3. The reason for attacking the shepherd at times could be just as a way to scatter the sheep

The shepherd and Sheep metaphorically refers to a leader and the followers and it should not be lost on us that a Leader is referred to as a Shepherd. We know that a Shepherd exists on account of the flock of sheep and the repute of the Shepherd is determined by the well-being of the flock

According to the Oxford dictionary, a leader is someone who leads or commands a group. Most of us play the role of a leader in different spheres of our lives; it could be as limited as being the leader of a family of three or as expansive as being the leader of a multi-national organisation. For some others, they have multiple leadership roles; being a father, a club president, head of a department etc.

The failure or success of a group is primarily dependent on the leader and not just the leadership style. There are bad leaders, good leaders, great leaders and effective leaders.

A bad leader is that person who is not able to muster the collective ability of the group to achieve the goal. A good leader is able to achieve the goal of the group but little else afterwards. A great leader is that one that is able to achieve the goal and impact on the lives of members of the group. The effective leader not only exceeds the goals of the group but gains total commitment and loyalty of the group.

After reading about the life of David several times in the Bible and being awed at his accomplishments, I decided to do an in-depth study into his character; how did he relate with the people he led, what attracted people to him with such deep sense of loyalty?

David, in the Bible is not presented with any airs of nobility, righteousness or overt spirituality around him, yet he is one of the most accomplished persons in the Bible.

We see David presented as an outlaw, liar, seducer, murderer, lover etc. He is depicted as an ordinary imperfect personality which makes him readily relate able; if he could have achieved all he did despite all these flaws, then we are without excuse.

It was David who established Israel into the great nation that God intended it to be. Prior to his kingship, the twelve tribes of Israel operated along tribal lines and their real loyalties were towards their tribesmen instead of a united entity called

Israel. There were several inter-tribal feuds such as when the tribe of Benjamin was decimated because of their transgression against the Levite traveller (Judges 20). After the coronation of Saul, he was still not accepted by all the tribes. Saul as a matter of fact reigned over a very weak kingdom as the Philistines were still in control of large territories of the land that was to be Israel. David not only conquered the old enemy, but expanded the territories of Israel and united the people behind him.

The Chosen One

Our first introduction to David is in 1 Samuel 16; here David comes out as the least esteemed in his family and the last of eight brothers.

The Prophet Samuel, having received instruction from God, travelled to Bethlehem with the intention to sacrifice unto The Lord. He met with Jesse and proceeded to invite him to the sacrifice along with "his sons". Jesse had eight boys, but went to the sacrifice with the seven older ones. Though, Samuel had not told Jesse the other reason for his presence in Bethlehem, the instruction to Jesse was however clear that he should come along with all of his boys. As a father, I would have taken all my children for such a momentous occasion; apart from the opportunity to be a partaker in the sacrifice and thereby learn some invaluable lessons, it would also have been a great honour to dine with such a great statesman as Samuel, but Jesse did not take along his youngest son. It would have been understandable if the boy was too young to appreciate the importance of such an event, but this was not the case as David at this time was about 17 years old.

All the seven brothers were presented to Samuel without any of them being chosen, it would have been expected that Jesse would then quickly send for his youngest son so that his household would not miss out on the honour. Instead, it took the insistence of the prophet for David to be presented *"...And Samuel said unto Jesse, Send and fetch him: for we will not sit down till he come hither."*

A Shepherd at Heart

The next thing we got to know about David was that he kept his father's sheep. In verse 11, Jesse finally introduced him as the youngest of his sons left behind to keep the sheep. This is an impressive responsibility to have at such a young age; whilst all his older brothers were at the sacrifice, David was trusted with the care of the sheep. Further on in Chapter 17, David talks about his prowess whilst keeping his father's sheep.

> *"Your servant used to keep his father's sheep, and when a lion or a bear came and took a lamb out of the flock, I went out after it and struck it, and delivered the lamb from its mouth; and when it arose against me, I caught it by its beard, and struck and killed it."*

This is a very remarkable account, which tells us that David was a young man who took his responsibilities seriously, with courage and was able to overcome such daunting challenges.

Multi-Skilled

We do not know of the right chronological order, but in Chapter 16, we got to know more about David as being a skilled musician amongst so many other virtues.

> *"Then one of the servants answered and said, "Look, I have seen a son of Jesse the Bethlehemite, who is skilful in playing, a mighty man of valour, a man of war, prudent in speech, and a handsome person; and the Lord is with him"* (verse 18).

David was invited to play the harp to help King Saul get over his demons. This was an early introduction to Music Therapy from the Bible. It wasn't just about being able to play the harp, but the spiritual environment created with the playing was what brought the healing virtue.

We also got to know later on that David was a chief Psalmist as he composed a considerable number of the Psalms in the Bible. Some of them were from his trials and travails, others from his everyday experiences whilst most were praises to exalt the name of God.

The testimony concerning David was also that he was prudent in speech. This showed that David was someone of great discernment, perception, intelligence and understanding; he was also apt in teaching others.

Able Leader

Being called a "man of valour" gives us a glimpse of the sort of leadership qualities that David had. Valour speaks of his strength, organisational efficiency, wealth and followership; these were apparently evident to all who observed him even from such early years.

Courageous

Perhaps what is best known about David and generally acknowledged as his greatest feat was the killing of Goliath.

Goliath was described as a giant nearly ten feet in height, dressed in heavy armour from head to toe. He had come out from the camp of the Philistines to challenge a champion of the Israelites to a one to one combat. However, we are told that Saul and the entire Israelite army were terrified and lost all hope. David had arrived at the Israelite camp on an errand for his father, being too young to join up with the army; he had stayed back at home to keep the sheep whilst his three oldest brothers were in the army.

When David was in the camp delivering his father's message to his brothers, Goliath came out from the Philistine's camp to once again issue the same challenge for a champion to come from Israel to face him in a one to one combat. Another part to David's personality was brought to the fore; he asked the soldiers around him what the reward would be for the person who defeats Goliath. Here, we get to see David as a fearless person who was ready to step up and undertake a task the most seasoned of the Israelite soldier was too scared to contemplate. Also, David was interested in the reward; he had expectations, he wasn't going to offer free service, he wanted the exact terms of the contract.

The rest of the story is commonly known, in that David defeated Goliath with just one stone thrown from his slingshot. David's life immediately changed after this; he became a general in King Saul's army, a son-in-law to the King, probably the most popular man in Israel with songs composed in his honour which unfortunately became a cause of deep-seated hatred from the King.

Henceforth, King Saul's life mission turned to eliminating David from the surface of the earth. After several unsuccessful attempts on his life by Saul, David ran away to seek refuge amongst the sworn enemies of the Israelites.

An Archetypal Leader

The next phase in David's life thus began as recorded in 1 Samuel 22:1-2,

> *"David therefore departed from there and escaped to the cave of Adullam. So when his brothers and all his father's house heard it, they went down there to him. And*

everyone who was in distress, everyone who was in debt, and everyone who was discontented gathered to him. So he became captain over them. And there were about four hundred men with him."

David raised a personal army of four hundred men, but these were not the sort of men that anybody would want to start an army with. They were in all sense and purpose a collection of the outcast of society, men who would be despised by others and lacking in the right sort of motivation.

But David continued to lead his band of disgruntled elements and turned them into a fierce fighting force, moving from city to city and leading raids against cities of nomads who harassed the Jews. He also led a dispirited army successfully against the Amalekites who had invaded the city of Ziklag where David was encamped and had taken away the families of all his men. This band of men whom David had built in the course of his exile years became the core of his army when David eventually became King over the whole of Israel. David continued to fight battles against the Philistines after he became King of Israel, and in three battles he forced the Philistines out of Israel.

David then began a campaign of takeover with Israelites neighbours on the East bank of Jordan. He fought with and defeated the Moabites, the Edomites, the Ammonites and the Arameans. David extended the Kingdom of Israel over both sides of the Jordan River, as far as the Mediterranean sea. There was no record of David's army ever being defeated in battle.

How exactly did David achieve such awesome feat with an army that started as a band of disgruntled men?

An Inspirational Leader

I believe that apart from the grace of God that was on his life and the divine mandate that David had, many of his victories came from the deep sense of loyalty that he commanded amongst his men. An example of this loyalty and commitment is seen in the story recounted in 2 Samuel 23:13-17,

> *"Then three of the thirty chief men went down at harvest time and came to David at the cave of Adullam. And the troop of Philistines encamped in the Valley of Rephaim. David was then in the stronghold, and the garrison of the Philistines was then in Bethlehem. And*

David said with longing "Oh, that someone would give me a drink of the water from the well of Bethlehem, which is by the gate!" So the three mighty men broke through the camp of the Philistines, drew water from the well of Bethlehem that was by the gate, and took it and brought it to David. Nevertheless he would not drink it, but poured it out to the LORD. And he said, "Far be it from me, O LORD, that I should do this! Is this not the blood of the men who went in jeopardy of their lives?" Therefore he would not drink it. These things were done by the three mighty men."

David just expressed a desire and the three men took it up as a mission, more or less a suicide mission. They went through the camp of the dreaded Philistines, just to get water from the well at Bethlehem for David to drink. Drinking the water had no tactical value whatsoever, but the men were ready to risk their lives just to grant a desire of the man they had decided to follow. These were the things that set apart the men that David was leading and it all comes from the leadership skills of the man David.

During the course of this book, I have looked at the various things David did to pass the message to his men. There is a lot to learn from him and by practising the lessons that have been drawn out, you can also be on your way to becoming an effective leader.

CHAPTER 1

Be Discerning

"Then the men of David said to him, "This is the day of which the LORD said to you, 'Behold, I will deliver your enemy into your hand, that you may do to him as it seems good to you.'" And David arose and secretly cut off a corner of Saul's robe. 6. And he said to his men, "The LORD forbid that I should do this thing to my master, the LORD'S anointed, to stretch out my hand against him, seeing he is the anointed of the LORD" (1 Samuel 24:4, 6).

In this passage, David was a fugitive, running away from Saul. He was operating as a guerrilla from the mountains in the wilderness. He avoided the major cities, as he knew the people would betray him to Saul.

At the beginning of Chapter 24, some people had approached Saul to let him know where David and his men were hiding. On being told the location, Saul took three thousand of his finest warriors to hunt down David. When Saul and his men reached the wilderness where David was supposed to be hiding, Saul needed to relieve himself. He saw a cave up ahead and he headed straight for the cave. Unknown to him nor to any of his men, he was walking straight into David's hands as David and his men were hiding inside the very same cave.

Saul must have walked in alone and after walking a few meters into the cave, he took off his robe folded it on one side and then bent down to relieve himself. All along, as soon as he entered the cave he had been watched by David and his men. These men could not believe their eyes as their enemy was walking in directly to where they hid. There was no better suggestion that this had been orchestrated by God, all David had to do was to kill Saul and the chief protagonist of their troubles will be done away with. David's leadership team urged him to strike quickly and mortally. But he declined their suggestion and instead, he stealthily approached where Saul was, passed by him, picked up Saul's folded robe and cut off a part of the skirt.

Watched by his dumbfounded men, David crept back to them and explained that it was wrong for him to strike down a man that had been anointed by God to be King.

David's men had offered a heartfelt suggestion to David on a genuine and sure way of ending the situation with Saul. All David had to do was to kill Saul, or let them do it on his behalf. It was an opportunity too good to be missed. David however could see a bigger picture based on his knowledge and experience with God.

Take Insightful Actions

A leader needs to see things differently from others, either from a strategic point of view or simply based on knowledge. You cannot afford to fall into the same mistakes as your subordinates.

David had deeper spiritual insight because he was a direct representative of God; he had been anointed and was now operating at a higher level in things of the spirit.

Saul had also been anointed, but it is not just a matter of the anointing because Saul fell short several times. He did not rise up to the level expected of him as an anointed king.

David saw the situation with Saul as one beyond a personal issue of Saul wanting to kill him, he saw beyond the obvious and brought God into the situation. He could have been angry with God and reasoned that if God was in the situation, He should have prevented him from being hunted by Saul.

Joseph demonstrated this rare insight in one of his encounters with his brothers after he had been sold into slavery and then emerging as a ruler in Egypt. In Genesis 45:3-8,

> *"Then Joseph said to his brothers, "I am Joseph; does my father still live?" But his brothers could not answer him, for they were dismayed in his presence. And Joseph said to his brothers, "Please come near to me." So they came near. Then he said: "I am Joseph your brother, whom you sold into Egypt. "But now, do not therefore be grieved or angry with yourselves because you sold me here; for God sent me before you to preserve life." "For these two years the famine has been in the land, and there are still five years in which there will be neither plowing nor harvesting." "And*

God sent me before you to preserve a posteriority for you in the earth, and to save your lives by a great deliverance." "So now it was not you who sent me here, but God; and He has made me a father to Pharaoh, and Lord of all his house, and a ruler throughout all the land of Egypt."

Imagine if Joseph had not understood this, but instead had ordered his brothers to be killed in revenge for all the agony they had made to befall him. God's plan for the preservation of Israel could have suffered a setback.

Enhanced Knowledge

A great leader will always seek for personal improvement through learning, while distinguishing himself intellectually. Devote time to reading and study in your specialized area, associated fields and generally too. You should always try to be a step ahead of your subordinates.

A leader should always be on top of his game; you don't need to be a specialist in all areas but you should be able to process facts and figures with a level of understanding that will stand you out.

Strategic Vs. Tactical Solutions

The leader sets the vision from which objectives and strategies are derived. Where there is no vision, there is a lack of direction and purposes are defeated. Vision stems from deep insight and this is what forms the building block for any institution or team. A vision is for the long term, it is not just about solving the immediate problem.

Understanding the interplay between long-term strategic objectives and short-term wins is an important leadership skill. David could have killed Saul in this instance and achieved a short-term win but would have suffered the consequences later. There are a lot of short-term and immediate solutions to the challenges a leader would face that are attractive and logical, but become detrimental in the longer term.

In my marketing career, I have come across several instances where sales volumes are declining or not reaching the expected targets and a need for an intervention arises. The default position by my colleagues in the sales function is usually to implement some form of 'sales promotion'. Oftentimes, the proposed sales promotion would be adequate and effective in addressing the current problem but I have rejected several of such, much to the chagrin of my colleagues. I would then have to explain that some of these solutions though might lead to a turnaround in current fortunes but might result in longer term damage to the equity of the brand as they are not in line with the positioning of the brand. It is also noteworthy that addressing a particular situation does not always deal with the underlying issue that led to such a situation. The right thing to do is to always fix the underlying issue and this requires a strategic mind-set.

In a family, the father as the leader of the home should set a vision for his family; this includes the children's educational, moral, social and spiritual development. He studies his children and understands their talents and gifts; he will use these to help them develop. He puts measures in place to ensure his children get a head-start in life.

It is recorded that the patriarch of the Kennedy family had a vision of wanting his boys to rule and he went about to order their lives around crystallising this vision. JFK is regarded as one of the great leaders of the United States, but the building blocks of becoming this were laid by his father.

Training Instead Of Rebuke

David did not rebuke his servants for their suggestion; rather he turned the situation into an opportunity for training and offered explanation. He did not ridicule them for making such an ungodly suggestion but used the opportunity to teach them about the ways of God. It would have been in his interest to kill Saul but he would have violated the principles of God by touching His anointed. Leaders should use every opportunity to develop and train their subordinates.

Oftentimes, subordinates offer suggestions based on their limited view of a situation and based on the information available to them or from their point of view, these opinions are valid and rational within context. It is important not to offhandedly dismiss such suggestions. To be a great leader, you should not rebuke your subordinates for being silly or belittle such opinions; by so doing you could destroy the confidence and initiative of those subordinates.

When Absalom rejected the counsel of Ahitophel in favour of that of Hushai in 1 Samuel 17, we are told that Ahitophel went home and committed suicide. He would surely not have killed himself purely because of a rejected counsel but it must have been the manner of the rejection that drove him to such an act

KING DAVID - MASTER Class

CHAPTER 2

Be Honourable

"And he said unto his men, The LORD forbid that I should do this thing unto my master, the LORD'S anointed, to stretch forth mine hand against him, seeing he is the anointed of the LORD" (1 Samuel 24:6).

When David crept back to his men in the cave after cutting off a piece of Saul's robe, he said something very profound; that he could not strike someone who had been anointed by God. David was not looking at the injustice that had been meted out to him by Saul, he looked beyond himself and focused on the law of God as seen in 1 Chronicles 16:22,

"Touch not mine anointed, and do my prophets no harm."

It could have been easy to manipulate the law; he could have cited self-defence or lied that it was an accident.

David did not take unfair advantage over his enemy; he did not kick him whilst he was down. David saw in Saul a reigning King rather than a forsaken leader. He could have exploited the troubles of Saul to his advantage; Saul was insecure, he was tormented by an evil spirit and he was clearly not the strong leader that Israel desired.

Fight Fair

By letting go of such an opportunity to strike down Saul, a clear message was being sent out to David's men that he is an honourable man. They would not have to be looking over their shoulders with David. They could be assured that David would also not turn against them nor exploit their weaknesses to his advantage.

You will always get several opportunities to profit from the misfortune of others, but it is a true test of character to be able to forgo such opportunities and fight fair.

Why would David let such an opportunity pass him by?

It was because David was secure in his position. This might seem odd, as he had actually fallen from grace to grass. He was now a fugitive, no longer the Captain in Saul's army, no longer the Son-in-law sitting at the King's table. He also could not be sure of the level of support he had amongst the Israelites who had sang his praises a few years ago. David's confidence was not in all of these external trappings or affirmation, his assurance was based on the anointing several years before by Samuel and the proclamation that he would be King. Saul had become king by divine permission and naturally the process of succession should have been through his lineage. God had however intervened and had chosen David to replace Saul.

When you derive your legitimacy as a leader from a position of credibility and not that you had schemed your way to the top or appointed fraudulently, you will have no reason to be insecure.

It is considered good management practice to exploit the weakness of our competitors or opponents, however a better way to being a great leader is to leverage on our strength rather than the weakness of others.

Feel Secured

As a husband, you should be secured in your position as the head of the house; a situation where a husband is always demanding for respect from his family shows that he is not fulfilling his role as the leader of the family. It does not matter if the wife is more educated or earns more; the father of the house should never feel threatened. Your value as the head of the house cannot be quantified in just monetary value or reduced to level of educational attainment. There should be no competition in the house between the husband and wife because the two roles are distinct and if the husband focuses on his leadership role, whatever his wife achieves will always be seen as complementary.

Husbands should never feel threatened of their position in the house even when they might be down financially or when the wife is earning more. Some wives do exploit such situations and use available opportunities to belittle the husband. It is a demonstration of poor leadership if the husband takes offence in such instances and starts to look for his own opportunities to get back at his wife by utilizing her weaknesses or other tactical advantages. David's focus was on the ordained relationship; Saul was the anointed King of Israel and regardless of what he was doing David knew that he would be in transgression if he struck him down. The husband should also focus on the covenant relationship and know that he is the leader; that the wife is not playing out her role does not create an excuse for the husband to retaliate. As the saying goes, "two wrongs do not make a right."

KING DAVID - MASTER Class

CHAPTER 3

Have A Sense Of Self-Worth

"David sent ten young men; and David said to the young men, "Go up to Carmel, go to Nabal, and greet him in my name. "And thus you shall say to him who lives in prosperity: 'Peace be to you, peace to your house, and peace to all that you have! 'Now I have heard that you have shearers. Your shepherds were with us, and we did not hurt them, nor was there anything missing from them all the while they were in Carmel. 'Ask your young men, and they will tell you. Therefore let my young men find favor in your eyes, for we come on a

feast day. Please give whatever comes to your hand to your servants and to your son David' " (1 Samuel 25:5–8).

Whilst David was hiding out in the wilderness, a group of shepherds minding the sheep of a rich man based in Maon called Nabal came under his protection. David and his men did their best in looking after the shepherds of Nabal and no harm came upon the men or the flock. A while later, David heard that Nabal was preparing a feast and with his own supplies running low, he sent some of his men to Nabal. David knew Nabal could afford to spare some provision, for he was identified as a man living in prosperity. David was not expecting to just receive free hand-outs; he had rendered valuable service to Nabal. In asking the young men to greet Nabal in his name, it should be expected that Nabal would know who David is. David made sure he specified to Nabal the sort of services he had rendered but that he was now soliciting in peace and for Nabal to show favor.

Place A Value On Yourself

David might have been wrong in making a demand from Nabal for the services he had rendered to him. The lesson here however was that David had a sense of self-worth; he did not see himself as just a vagabond roaming the wilderness. He had offered free services but it was not cheap, which was why he told his servants to tell Nabal that "Your shepherds were with us, and we did not hurt them, nor was there anything missing from them all the while they were in Carmel"

A great leader will always have a sense of self-worth because people will not esteem you higher than the way you perceive yourself. The way you are perceived will also determine the value and expectations that people have of you.

In marketing it is commonly known that consumers associate price with quality, so the higher the price, the higher the perceived quality and hence value. No matter the quality of an item, if it falls below an expected price, the value associated to that item by the consumer also drops.

Pastors will only be too familiar with this scenario. When a Pastor goes out to minister and then decides to share exactly the same message, with the same examples as had been shared with his home congregation, the results are sometimes startling different. The same message to two different congregations produces far better results in manifestation, faith and testimonies amongst the hosting congregation. This is usually because the hosting congregation has more expectations of the guest minister due to a higher level of estimation. The home congregation has become too familiar with their Pastor and do not have as much regard for him as they would for a visiting Pastor. So, in order for the Pastor to continue to be a blessing to his congregation, he will need to increase his self-worth. In this case however, it is not about the Pastor exalting himself, as he is a vessel in God's hand; it is about people having respect for the call of God on his life and the commission he has received.

Self-worth of a leader should however go beyond financial terms, so that even if you work for free, you will work with dignity and excellence. You should be able to boast like David that no one was hurt and nothing was missing, that is, I did not enrich myself at your expense.

Allow For Appreciation

The assistance David and his men had rendered to Nabal was over and beyond the normal course of duty. David had no obligation to protect the Shepherds of Nabal as himself and his men were also fugitives trying to stay alive. David had probably offered the protection out of the good nature of his heart.

The motivation for offering the help should not primarily be because of the reward, but there is nothing wrong in expecting a reward for your services. More often than not, the reward will not come from the exact source where you have sown so you need to be on the alert for the harvest. In the story about Nabal and David, we later found out that it was Nabal's wife who brought the provision to David. She did not know, as at the time she was preparing the provision, that David and his men were, in fact, on their way to attack Nabal.

On an emotional level, leaders always have a need for appreciation. The level of appreciation usually serves as reassurance to the leader that he is on the right track. Do not give the humble "Don't mention it" response when being appreciated. People do not always feel that they are paying you back for your services when appreciating you, it is only a means of expressing their love. It also helps the people you are leading to feel connected to you, as transactions should be a two-way process; it is unhealthy when it is just one-way.

> *"Whoever goes to war at his own expense? Who plants a vineyard and does not eat of its fruit? Or who tends a flock and does not drink of the milk of the flock? Do I say*

these things as a mere man? Or does not the law say the same also? For it is written in the law of Moses, "You shall not muzzle an ox while it treads out the grain." Is it oxen God is concerned about? Or does He say it altogether for our sakes? For our sakes, no doubt, this is written, that he who plows should plow in hope, and he who threshes in hope should be partaker of his hope. If we have sown spiritual things for you, is it a great thing if we reap your material things? If others are partakers of this right over you, are we not even more? Nevertheless we have not used this right, but endure all things lest we hinder the gospel of Christ. Do you not know that those who minister the holy things eat of the things of the temple, and those who serve at the altar partake of the offerings of the altar? Even so the Lord has commanded that those who preach the gospel should live from the gospel" (1 Corinthians 9:7-14)

Do Not Exploit

In as much as it is good to expect a reward or recognition as a leader, such a privilege must not be exploited or abused. A leader should never have the mind-set of expecting something for nothing.

In Genesis 23:1-18, we read of an encounter between Abraham and the men of Canaan after the death of Sarah. Abraham wanted a place in which to bury Sarah and he approached the sons of Heth to purchase a burial place. The men of the place were honoured to have Abraham in their midst and acknowledged him as a mighty prince amongst them, he was offered the choicest place in their burial ground. Abraham rather wanted a place of his own and requested for a specific cave belonging to one of the men, Ephron the Hittite. Ephron was glad to give out his land to Abraham and offered it free of charge. Abraham however insisted on paying the full price for the property and he promptly did so, on the spot. Several other leaders would have only been too glad to take advantage of the free offer and thereby lose respect.

Don't expect freebies to be delivered to you from followers. You need to have wisdom to know how to balance between accepting rewards and exploiting the vulnerability or adoration of followers.

Whatsoever you receive as a leader must be acknowledged and appreciated, at the very least. In

Philippians 4, Paul acknowledged the generosity of the Philippian church and mentioned in verse 17 that he received the gifts not so much because he needed the gifts but as a way of blessing them. He was confident that there would be fruits yielding to their account because of the seeds they had sown.

Reward Fairly

The same principle of a leader having a sense of self-worth also has a flip side; the leader should also place a value on his/her team members for their labour.

David did not have an agreement with Nabal to be remunerated for the service he had rendered in protecting his flock and shepherds. Nabal was therefore at liberty to decline giving anything to David, but David's expectation was not based on any binding agreement but on what is fair. It is this same principle that should guide any leader; give remuneration that is fair based on the value derived from the service.

A leader should offer remuneration that is fair and commensurate; the same way that you have expectations of your workers or followers to put in their best into the assigned tasks so must you remunerate them fairly. Your workers have an idea of their worth or the value of their services, when you do not meet their expectations they will not be pleased. There are always unrealistic expectations which you cannot meet or shouldn't meet as a good manager of resources but you should never take advantage of people's service to you.

There are ways in which you remunerate for good service over and beyond the salary that is paid; recognition of efforts at times could be all that is required, awards also helps, celebrating achievements or personal milestones are also handy tools.

Service in the ministry is often voluntary and more often than not, the level of commitment and loyalty is always outstanding. It is a sign of bad leadership when these workers are taken for granted. Since the service is voluntary, they are not expecting to be paid but it is only fair that they are rewarded. Find creative ways to reward the people supporting you.

CHAPTER 4

Demand Competency

"So David said to Abner, "Are you not a man? And who is like you in Israel? Why then have you not guarded your lord the king? For one of the people came in to destroy your lord the king. "This thing that you have done is not good. As the LORD lives, you deserve to die, because you have not guarded your master, the LORD's anointed. And now see where the king's spear is, and the jug of water that was by his head" (1 Samuel 26:15-16).

This was a second encounter where David had the opportunity to kill Saul.

Saul had been told by the Ziphites that David was hiding in the hill of Hachilah and again, Saul chose three thousand of his finest soldiers to pursue David. When Saul approached the wilderness where David and his men were based, David got to know about it and he sent spies out to discover where Saul was setting up his camp. When David was told where Saul had set up camp, David and one of his trusted lieutenants went over to Saul's camp. They arrived at Saul's camp by night time and scoped it out. They soon discovered where Saul himself was located. Lo and behold, Saul was fast asleep surrounded by his army and next to him was his army commander, Abner.

David and his aide were able to approach where Saul was sleeping undetected and got right up to Saul. Abishai, who had followed David offered to strike Saul dead (obviously remembering that David would not do so himself) but David restrained him. Again, he explained to him that it was wrong to kill an anointed King.

David however, chose to take some mementoes to prove his infiltration into Saul's camp. He took Saul's spear and his jug of water lying just beside Saul's head.

David was clearly appalled that Abner the army commander had also been sleeping and an enemy was able to infiltrate the camp and get to striking distance of Saul. This was totally unacceptable to David.

It was either that Abner was not taking his job seriously or he did not know what was expected of him. He had not set up the camp defences to prevent such an infiltration. He might have set up sentries to prevent a full scale attack but his primary focus was supposed to be protection of Saul's life.

It could be argued that David had no right to scold Abner as he was someone else's aide and ideally a leader's scope of responsibility is to his own team. In this case however, it should be recognized that David had been a general in Saul's army, he still owed allegiance and regarded Saul as his King, though he was being hunted as a fugitive. He knew Abner and what his role in Saul's army should be and this was what he demanded of Abner (a study of the life of Abner reveals several flaws and hardly anything distinguishing in his career or about his character).

Always Give Job Descriptions

David spoke to Abner with regard to not living up to his responsibility. It is essential that a leader must let his subordinates know their specific responsibilities. It is important that you let your subordinates have a clear and unambiguous job description. Subordinates should have an understanding of one primary reason for their roles; some definition of their utmost priority.

It is a demonstration of bad leadership skill for members of your team to be ignorant of their topmost specific responsibilities.

In a football team, there is supposed to be one goalkeeper, a certain number of defenders, the midfielders and then the attackers. The goalkeeper knows that it is his role to keep goal and that is his major contribution to the team, not to take free kicks or be making the throw-ins. The Manager cannot field two goalkeepers no matter how much he likes both of them; neither can he pack his team with attackers without defenders. Apart from conforming to the rules of the game, the team should be set up to attack and to defend. The attackers have to do their job as well as the defenders doing theirs. The attackers do fall back to help the defenders when the opposing team is with the ball, but their primary purpose in the team is to score goals.

In homes, it is good to assign responsibilities to the children and to let them know each person's specific responsibility. It could be as simple. but as specific as telling child A that it is his responsibility to ensure that the doors are always properly locked up every night before bed time.

Assign Responsibilities Responsibly

There are two major considerations to consider before appointing people to fill roles; first is the competence of the candidate and the second is the availability or necessity of such a role.

In churches, appointment or ordination into leadership positions should not be based on length of service in the ministry or loyalty. Elders should be chosen based on competence for the role and not as a reward for service.

People should not be appointed to positions first before responsibilities are thought of or created for them. It should be that there are responsibilities that demand attention, and the right people for the job are sought out and placed in those positions. For example: any person who goes by the title Pastor should have a congregation that he or she is responsible for. The Choir master does not have to be a Pastor nor the Church Treasurer.

Leadership is about assigning responsibilities to capable people. It should not be about awarding titles to please people.

In Acts 6:1-4, the seven men appointed were chosen to perform a given task.

> *"Now in those days, when the number of the disciples was multiplying, there arose a complaint against the Hebrews by the Hellenists, because their widows were neglected in the daily distribution. Then the twelve summoned the multitude of the disciples and said, "It is not desirable that we should leave the word of God and serve tables. "Therefore, brethren, seek out from among you seven men of good reputation, full of the Holy Spirit and wisdom, whom we may appoint over this business; "but we will give ourselves continually to prayer and to the ministry of the word."*

CHAPTER 5

Be A Loyalist

"And David and his men went up and raided the Geshurites, the Girzites, and the Amalekites. For those nations were the inhabitants of the land from of old, as you go to Shur, even as far as the land of Egypt. Whenever David attacked the land, he left neither man nor woman alive, but took away the sheep, the oxen, the donkeys, the camels, and the apparel, and returned and came to Achish. Then Achish would say, "Where have you made a raid today?" And David would say, "Against the southern area of Judah, or against the southern area of the Jerahmeelites, or

against the southern area of the Kenites." David would save neither man nor woman alive, to bring newsto Gath, saying, "Lest they should inform on us, saying, 'Thus David did.'" And thus was his behavior all the time he dwelt in the country of the Philistines. So Achish believed David, saying, "He has made his people Israel utterly abhor him; therefore he will be my servant forever" (1 Samuel 27:8–12).

After spending time wandering in the wilderness and being pursued by Saul, David decided to go and join up with the enemies of Israel. David went to meet Achish the son of Maoch, king of Gath for refuge. His main reason was that Saul would not be able to follow him into the land of the Philistines.

Achish the King of Gath accepted David and his men and on the request of David, Achish granted them the land of Ziklag to live in.

David, though living amongst the Philistines would still go out with his men to attack outlying cities of the Amalekites, but would tell Achish that he was attacking the cities of Judah.

David did not forsake old ties. He remained loyal to his country, Israel, despite seeking refuge with the enemy. David did not become a traitor to his people; this would ensure that his own men would not turn against him in the future.

Do Not Forget Old Ties

Most people who rise to positions of leadership start to forge new alliances in order to fit in and to be accepted; they turn their backs on old friendships and sometimes totally turn against these old acquaintances. Unlike David, they are ready to campaign against their old friends in order to curry favour with the new.

Old friends are those who are not prejudiced by the new position, they will be bold to tell you the truth. They are not awestruck by you, they will not be sycophants; always telling you what you want to hear

The old constituency would usually always be your strongest ally, if you carry them along.

It is a popular saying that no matter where you rise up to, never forget where you are coming from, because it is such memories that will keep you grounded.

You might ask, how do you handle the issue of jealousy amongst former colleagues who have not been as fortunate?

The truth is that jealousy will most likely be subsumed when former colleagues are made to share of your success, feel they are a part and will be favoured by it.

Do Not Disparage Former Allies

Another popular saying is "not to bite the finger that is feeding you or that has fed you". In politics, most times you have politicians cross carpeting to rival parties and then start to tear down the party from which they have just exited. Not only do such politicians demonstrate a complete lack of guiding ideology, but they forget the benefits that had been derived from their membership of the previous party. These are signs of weak leadership attributes; it means that such persons could easily turn from their current beliefs the moment there is another attractive inducement elsewhere.

If you are part of an organisation and you do not agree with some of their beliefs or principles, there is nothing wrong with speaking out and leaving, if need be. The Bible says in Amos 3:3

"Can two walk together, unless they are agreed?"

When you do have to speak about such an organisation, limit yourself to the personal grievances or disagreements and not start to destroy former allies.

A leader cannot build an enduring legacy or gain true followership by slandering his rivals, especially when that leader has been a part of the rival organisation.

CHAPTER 6

Be Decisive

> *"Now David was greatly distressed, for the people spoke of stoning him, because the soul of all the people was grieved, every man for his sons and his daughters. But David strengthened himself in the LORD his God"* (1 Samuel 30:6).

David had led his men to go along with the Philistines to battle but were turned back as the other Philistine kings were uncomfortable with having David and his men in their midst.

When David and his men returned to their city, Ziklag, they were confronted by a calamity; in their absence the Amalekites had invaded Ziklag and razed it to the ground with fire. All the women and children had been captured and led away.

All the returning men inclusive of David were devastated at the loss and started to cry out loudly. The men could not contain their grief and laid it all at David's feet. They were going to lynch David and stone him to death.

Take Charge

David had to pick himself up and act as a leader in a time of crisis. He did not cede authority or responsibility to any of his followers.

Leaders are made in times of crises and are proven by adversity. Most people can lay claim to having the capacity to lead, but it is when the sea is rough and the wind is strong that the wheat is separated from the chaff.

A genuine leader possesses courage and will make decisions, not unambiguous statements. This is the time when the team is looking up for direction and the way the crisis is managed will either make or break the team.

This is not to say that great leaders don't suffer defeats, but at least they stand up to be counted when it matters most. It is not the time for the deputies to start making decisions. People want to hear the voice and opinion of the leader at times such as these. It is not coincidental that it is the leaders who led their nations to victory during the times of war and crises that are most revered today; the Abraham Lincolns, Winston Churchill, etc.

There is nothing as bad as a silent leader when things have gone wrong.

Be Open To Criticism

It is also instructive that David did not hold the intent of the men to stone him against them. What they intended to do was a clear case of insurrection for which they should have been punished. David was able to distinguish between emotional reactions and a deliberate rational action. Without the emotions, the men would never have thought of stoning David. Leaders must be able to accommodate criticism and opposition and turn these into opportunities. The same men that started out wanting to stone David were the same set of people that David roused up to chase after the Amalekites that had committed the atrocious act.

Leaders should be able to detach themselves from criticism and not always take it personal; when they do this they will be able to appreciate the message. Agreed that not all criticism is well intentioned, but at the same time most are sincere expressions of an aggrieved mind.

Do Not Pass The Blame

In this situation, David did not try to pass the blame for the calamity unto someone else; he did not look for a scapegoat to blame. He could have torn into his army captain for not ensuring that the town of Ziklag was well defended whilst the others went out to war or he could have accused the Philistines of tricking them out so that Ziklag would be defenceless for the Amalekites to attack. Most times, when a situation of great loss occurs leaders take too much time in analysing the situation to look for someone to blame. This is not the time to be setting up a committee to recommend appropriate action. David took the situation up personally and as time was of the essence, he got his men into action as soon as he got direction.

Manage Change

A true leader has to be able to manage change; the composition of the team will not always be consistent, there will be times of full motivation and other times of demoralisation, there will be times of full loyalty and other times of lukewarmness. The same men that had gladly followed David to join up with the Philistine army and who would have given their lives for his now spoke of stoning him to death. If David had not handled the situation well, they would have executed their intentions. As a leader, how do you handle the situation when things are not looking rosy or when situations have turned upside down? How do you react when the enemy is gaining the upper hand, when sales are down, when attendance in church is down, when the finances have dried up or when there is a battle to be won? Do you further demoralise the team with your cluelessness, weaknesses or obstinacy and in the process lose your followership.

KING DAVID - MASTER Class

CHAPTER 7

Be Compassionate

"Then they found an Egyptian in the field, and brought him to David; and they gave him bread and he ate, and they let him drink water. And they gave him a piece of a cake of figs and two clusters of raisins. So when he had eaten, his strength came back to him; for he had eaten no bread nor drunk water for three days and three nights" (1 Samuel 30:11-13).

David had roused his men to pursue after the Amalekites; there were six hundred men in all but they were determined in following David to recover their wives, children and possessions that had been carried off by the Amalekites.

It is interesting that with such a determined focus and objective by the men, seeing a wounded and destitute Egyptian by the wayside, they still stopped to attend to him. They gave him bread to eat, a piece of a cake of figs and two clusters of raisins, as well as water to drink.

David demonstrated compassion to a destitute on the roadside though he had pressing needs of his own. The life of the Egyptian was not taken for granted, he was deemed important enough for the marching army to be halted in order that he might be attended to. To be able to put someone else's needs above your goals and objectives, more so when both needs seem to be totally unrelated, can only spring from a heart that is full of empathy.

As I stated in the intro about the man David, it is the strong sense of loyalty that he commanded amongst his men that made him the great leader he was. This strong followership was built as they observed his every action and decision. The message he sent across as they encountered this Egyptian and tended to his need was that every life was important to him; how reassuring that must have been to all his followers. To know that their leader would be touched by their physical, emotional or psychological needs would bring out the best in any follower.

Show Interest In Others

An effective leader is truly compassionate, feels the pain of others from the heart. People will not be able to give you their best when they are physically down or mentally disturbed.

There is a need to unharness the horses and let them feed and rest in order to replenish their strength. Leaders must understand the necessity to allow members of the team to unwind and replenish.

Leaders have to be sensitive to the mood and body languages of team members.

Several years ago, back in Nigeria before the days of mobile phones and as a Junior Manager in a Multi-national company, I was to make a two-day out-of-station trip with my head of department and another departmental head. Basically I was accompanying them on the trip as the errand runner, so I was expected to make all the things associated with the trip run smoothly. In my effort to please, I made arrangement to get to the airport as early as I could to purchase the tickets and other airport protocol. The day before the trip, I got home very late at about 12:30am and decided to leave my car parked in front of my house. I hardly ever park my car there because it was not a much secured place, but due to the fact that it was already so late and I would be leaving quite early I decided to take the risk. The following morning before dawn, I was up and ready to go and as I got out of the front door I noticed something was wrong with the car. On approach, I saw that the door was slightly ajar and as I reached the car my worst fears were confirmed, the car had been broken into and vandalised. Components had been stolen from the engine and it would not start. It was traumatic for me but I still needed to join the trip. I went over to a friend's place living in the same neighbourhood and had to drag him out of bed so early. I explained the situation to him and pleaded with him to help arrange for the car to be moved away to a safe place as I would be away on a trip for a few days in order to prevent further damage to the car. I then had to make my way to the airport by some other means. Needless to say, I got to the airport later than expected and Senior Managers were already waiting. My Head of Department was fuming and started tongue lashing me as soon as I showed up, letting me know how incompetent I was. I did not get any opportunity to explain the reason why I was late. All through the trip, she maintained a wall of silence and coldness. On return, three days later I got a heavily worded query on my desk asking me to respond immediately as to why further disciplinary action should not be taken against me. It was only then in my response to the query that I was able to state my side of the story and the car incidence. After my response, no further mention was made, no compassion expressed, no disciplinary action taken. I had not performed to the best of my abilities on that trip.

Maybe if my Head of Department had just asked me the reason why I was late and had listened to me before the trip, I could have been excused rather than becoming a liability or being less than effective.

At the same time, I recollect another line manager who would always put the welfare of the team up there alongside the deliverables. Several times when we were having quarterly results presentations to the Regional Manager, he would push the team to ensure no stones were left unturned. This involved working late hours in the office, but he would have ensured that we all booked into a hotel next to the office so that nobody would have to travel home at such late hours.

A leader who cares as much for the people as he does for the task at hand, is on the path to true greatness. You should care for the lives and livelihood of the people you are leading or that you come across. If a subordinate calls in sick, what is the first thought that flashes through your mind? Is it about the tasks that would be left undone, the targets that would be missed or the wellbeing of the sick team member? An organisation where the Human Resources Director is more concerned about what the staff policy says about sick days when an employee has been off, sick for a week or so, instead of visiting the sick employee should not expect any lasting loyalty.

Nobody Is Inconsequential

Several times in the gospel, we see Jesus being called to attend to various needs in the house of different individuals: Healing of Jairus's daughter in Matthew 9:18-26, healing the Centurion's servant in Matthew 8:5-13, raising Lazarus from the dead in John 11:1-44. In the story about Jairus' daughter, we see Jesus stop as he was on his way to Jairus' house because something else extraordinary had occurred. He stopped and asked for who it was that had touched Him because He knew power to heal had flowed out of Him. When the woman who did touch Him acknowledged that it was her and narrated the situation, her expectation and experience; Jesus confirmed her miracle. Jesus could have ignored the slight inconvenience and inconsequential episode in order to focus on the matter of healing the daughter of Jairus (a ruler of the synagogue), an important man, by all standards, that had approached Him openly. There was a huge crowd following to see what would happen at Jairus's house; this was a big opportunity to showcase His power and authority, so why stop over an incidence that nobody knew about.

> *"For we do not have a High Priest who cannot sympathize with our weaknesses, but was in all points tempted as we are, yet without sin"* (Hebrews 4:15).

Jesus does not set Himself apart from us; He sympathizes with us in every situation. That is why He would readily go to Jairus' house or the Centurion's house when requested. That is why we can still boldly come to Him today despite the fact that we are weak.

Pastors should not allow programmes and administrative commitments to take the place of ministering to people's need. Every member of the congregation is important and should be able to receive needed attention. There are large congregations where it is impossible for the Pastor to minister personally to everyone's need, but the necessary organizational structure can be put in place so that nobody will feel inconsequential. The Pastor, as Shepherd of the flock, will get to know who is in or out of the flock, thereby knowing the needs of the flock. Being an effective leader is not about the level of crowd worship and adulation received but about being able to respond to the needs of the people.

Jesus gave a testimony in John 17:12,

> *"While I was with them in the world, I kept them in Your name. Those whom You gave Me I have kept; and none of them is lost except the son of perdition, that the Scripture might be fulfilled."*

Jesus as the chief shepherd knew His flock and fought for them so that none was lost. He told Peter in Luke 22:31-32,

> *"And the Lord said, "Simon, Simon! Indeed, Satan has asked for you, that he may sift you as wheat. "But I have prayed for you, that your faith should not fail; and when you have returned to Me, strengthen your brethren."*

Pastors should fight for the lives of each member of their congregation and be able to give a similar sincere testimony like Jesus did; that none of them is lost. When members do err and say they are going to leave the church, the Pastor should be able to swallow his ego and fight for the soul of that member with genuine compassion, knowing that most people after leaving a church may end up not attending a church again. When people's lives do truly matter to you as a Pastor, you are becoming a genuine leader and not just a preacher in front of a large crowd.

Make It About Lives

Great leadership can be measured by the impact it makes on people's lives. The people being led can see an improvement in their standard of living and can say with confidence that their leader is working for their best interest. Their primary needs of welfare, security, housing etc. are being taken care of.

Political leaders sometimes use positive economic indices to showcase the impact of their leadership but when investigated deeply, such positive economic outlook is not reflected positively in the lives of the populace. Leadership is about lives and not the numbers. Economic growth should be reflected in better standard of living. It is the height of callousness when leaders turn a deaf ear to the cries of the people; if you cannot respond to their cries then you are not fit to lead them.

CHAPTER 8

Be Team Minded

"Then all the wicked and worthless men of those who went with David answered and said, "Because they did not go with us, we will not give them any of the spoil that we have recovered, except for every man's wife and children, that they may lead them away and depart." But David said, "My brethren, you shall not do so with what the LORD has given us, who has preserved us and delivered into our hand the troop that came against us. "For who will heed you in this matter? But as his part is who goes down to the battle,

so shall his part be who stays by the supplies; they shall share alike" (1 Samuel 30:23-24).

When David and his men were pursuing the Amalekites, about two hundred of the men were too weary to continue with the pursuit. The men had just returned from following the Philistine and then returned to Ziklag to meet the calamity. We were not told of how much time they had to rest or recover before David rounded them up again for the pursuit.

On reaching the Brook Besor, the two hundred men were just too exhausted to go across. David decided to have them stay behind whilst he continued with the rest of the men.

The four hundred men with David were able to completely defeat the Amalekites and they rescued all the women, children, flocks, livestock and many more besides. In triumph, they marched back towards their city but on reaching the Brook Besor, a problem arose. The two hundred men who had stayed behind came out to meet with the triumphant company but not all of the men who had gone into battle were happy to see them. These men told David that the men that had stayed behind should not share of the booty from their victory with the men that had gone to battle.

David however did not see things from their point of view, he ruled that they were all part of the same team and the men who went to battle will share of the loot alike as those who stayed behind.

Reward Fairly

David treated all his men equally; those that went to battle received the same reward as those that were too weak to go. Nobody was deemed as being of lesser value.

In major football competitions, every member of the winning team receives a medal, this includes the substitutes, the reserve players who probably didn't play a single minute throughout the tournament as well as the assistant coaches. As long as you are a registered member of the team, you are entitled to the same reward. At the 1994 FIFA world cup, a young Brazilian named Ronaldo was included in the team not so much for the contribution he would make to the squad, but for his expected contribution to future squads. Brazil won the tournament and Ronaldo received the same winner's medal as the more established players in the team.

Value Everyone's Contribution

It is important that leaders know how to value every member of the team, no matter the level of their contribution. There are people who are in the team just to make others happy and when the main players are happy, the team's success is guaranteed. You cannot have a team that consists of the same type of individuals, but each individual is valuable. A good leader will draw attention to the value every team member brings to the team rather than favour the supposedly stronger members over the weaker ones

This does not override the appraisal system available in most organisations where people are assessed according to achievements in personal Key Results Area. This sort of appraisal should be personal and it is the individual being assessed against his or her objectives and compensated based on efforts to meet the targets or objectives.

CHAPTER 9

Build Alliances

"Now when David came to Ziklag, he sent some of the spoil to the elders of Judah, to his friends, saying, "Here is a present for you from the spoil of the enemies of the LORD" to those who were in Bethel, those who were in Ramoth of the South, those who were in Jattir, those who were in Aroer, those who were in Siphmoth, those who were in Eshtemoa, those who were in Rachal, those who were in the cities of the Jerahmeelites, those who were in the cities of the Kenites those who were in Hormah, those who were in Chorashan, those who were in Athach, those who were in Hebron,

and to all the places where David himself and his men were accustomed to rove" (1 Samuel 30:26–29).

David distributed of his spoils of war to the leaders of Judah, thereby buying their indebtedness. He was looking to the future when he would have need of their goodwill and loyalty. Celebrate your victories, learn to be generous.

Promote Team Unity

A good leader strives to build harmony within the team by sharing the rewards and acknowledging the various direct and indirect contributions. You should not monopolize the whole limelight and refuse to share the glory with team members who played a role in the success, including acknowledging those whose roles were indirect

Seek Peace

It is also important to build alliances for the present and future. Success is easier to achieve in an environment of peace than in hostility. You do not have to be hostile to your competitors no matter how fierce the rivalry might be. Great leadership also involves seeking avenues for peace rather than war

> *"If it is possible, as much as depends on you, live peaceably with all men"* (Romans 12:18).

As part of a larger unit or organisation, you win valuable alliances by being favourable to the other departments or teams. When things are going well, reach out to the other teams with aids or different forms of helps. Heads of nations build regional alliances by being favourable to the surrounding nations and this should not always be from a selfish stand point.

Unite People For Strength

The church needs leaders that will start to build alliances amongst the different denominations to make the church a powerful force once again.

The devil learnt from what God did in Genesis 11:6-7,

> *"And the LORD said, "Indeed the people are one and they all have one language, and this is what they begin to do; now nothing that they propose to do will be withheld from them. "Come, let us go down and there confuse their language,*

that they may not understand one another's speech."

One of his weapons against the church to limit her effectiveness to achieving her goal is to confuse her language. There are now as many doctrines in the church as there are nations on the earth. If the church speaks with one language then just as God testified in Genesis, nothing she proposes to do will be withheld from her.

Leadership in the church needs to be building alliances to overcome polarisation into denominational factions which is limiting the effectiveness of the church. There is a common enemy for the church, but polarisation will lead to rivalry and all sorts of unhealthy competition; bigger than yours congregation, building, choir, more miracles, anointing etc.

CHAPTER 10

Justice For Impropriety

> *"So David said to him, "How was it you were not afraid to put forth your hand to destroy the LORD's anointed?" Then David called one of the young men and said, "Go near, and execute him!" And he struck him so that he died. So David said to him, "Your blood is on your own head, for your own mouth has testified against you, saying, 'I have killed the LORD's anointed'"* (2 Samuel 1:14–16).

In the last chapter of 1 Samuel, Saul and the Israelite army were at war against the Philistines. The Philistines had gained the upper hand and several of the men in Saul's army had been killed.

The Philistines started to chase after Saul and his sons; they succeeded in killing three of Saul's sons including Jonathan. Saul was also mortally wounded and did not want to fall into the hands of the Philistines so he asked his armour bearer to finish off the job. The armour bearer was however too fearful and could not kill Saul, so Saul took his sword and with his hands, he thrust the sword into himself.

The third day after these events, a man from Saul's camp approached David's camp in Ziklag and sought audience with David. He reported to David that Saul and Jonathan had been killed in battle and that he was actually the person who finished Saul off when he saw Saul mortally wounded. To buttress his case, he presented David with Saul's crown and bracelet.

To the man's utmost amazement, instead of David to jubilate over the death of his enemy, David tore off his clothes in anguish and started to weep for Saul, Jonathan and the army of Israel. After a whole day of mourning in the camp of David, David called the man who had brought the news over to him and instructed that the man be killed for daring to lift up his hands against a king of Israel.

David exacted maximum retribution for impropriety.

Implement Discipline

A leader should always be ready to enforce discipline, no matter whose ox is gored.

People sometimes flay David for this action because the man did not really kill Saul as he made it to sound like. Maybe David should not have carried out such an instant judgement, but should have waited and probably the truth would have been revealed that this man had not been the one who killed Saul. David clearly stated in this encounter that the man was to die because of what he had testified of, regardless of what he did or did not do. There are times when what you say carries more weight than what you actually did; because in life "Perception is reality". A leader should always be mindful of whatever perception is being created.

As the head of a family, discipline should never be compromised; no matter how much you love the children, there should be boundaries with consequences when those boundaries are crossed.

Pastors must also maintain firm discipline in church, doctrinal issues must be addressed firmly and without reservation. Erring members should know they will face the music for their impropriety without any form of favouritism. Truth in the church must never be compromised, a Pastor cannot be preaching a message that is different from what he practises or allows.

> *"But if I am delayed, I write so that you may know how you ought to conduct yourself in the house of God, which is the church of the living God, the pillar and ground of the truth"* (1 Timothy 3:15).

An experience in my early Christian life which I cannot forget happened in church on a particular Sunday. The Pastor went up on stage and told the whole congregation that he had a serious announcement to make. He called up a sister to the stage and told the church that he wanted to speak to her publicly as he had done so repeatedly in private without seeing the desired result. The sister had been reported to the Pastor by the wife of a man (not a member of the church) that the sister was having an affair with and after many entreaties the sister still persisted with the affair. To me, that was how to lay a standard as a leader on what you believe and stand for without compromise.

Do Not Compromise

We read in Galatians 2:11-14 of Paul confronting Peter due to what could be termed as acts of hypocrisy.

> *"Now when Peter had come to Antioch, I withstood him to his face, because he was to be blamed; for before certain men came from James, he would eat with the Gentiles; but when they came, he withdrew and separated himself, fearing those who were of the circumcision. And the rest of the Jews also played the hypocrite with him, so that even Barnabas was carried away with their hypocrisy. But when I saw that they were not straightforward about the truth of the gospel, I said to Peter before them all, "If you, being a Jew, live in the manner of Gentiles and not as the Jews, why do you compel Gentiles to live as Jews?"*

Earlier on in the same chapter, Paul had acknowledged Peter as one of the pillars of the church and part of the leadership that released him to work in the ministry. He was able to confront the very same Peter because of his zeal to defend the message that he had been entrusted with. We are not told of Peter reacting negatively to the challenge by Paul because in truth, both of them were subject to the leading of the Holy Spirit and it wasn't about who was senior.

The confrontation between Paul and Peter would probably not have been expected to happen in a corporate establishment because Paul was Peter's subordinate (considering the fact that Peter was with Jesus and was the first man to preach the gospel after the Pentecost at a time when Paul was still waging a war against Christians). Even less possible in the military, Paul would have been court-marshalled!

It is in such instances as these however that leadership traits are developed; the subordinate in the corporate environment or in the military who is ready to sacrifice his position in defence of a principle or justice is a leader in the making. It is expected that every other person would dance to the tune of the superiors. People like Nelson Mandela, Mahatma Ghandi, Martin Luther King etc. made such sacrifices for what they believed to be right.

CHAPTER 11

Place Value On Your Assets

"And David said, "Good, I will make a covenant with you. But one thing I require of you: you shall not see my face unless you first bring Michal, Saul's daughter, when you come to see my face." So David sent messengers to Ishbosheth, Saul's son, saying, "Give me my wife Michal, whom I betrothed to myself for a hundred foreskins of the Philistines" (2 Samuel 3:13-14).

After the death of Saul, Abner, the commander of Saul's army took Ishbosheth one of Saul's sons and made him king over the rest of Israel. By this time, David had been made king over the house of Judah.

The Israelite army commanded by Abner continued with the war against David and his men. Abner began to consolidate his position in the household of Saul and decided to take one of Saul's concubines as his. This action angered Ishbosheth and he challenged Abner for taking one of his father's concubines. Abner felt insulted and vowed to transfer allegiance to David.

He sent emissaries to David asking David for his allegiance and that he would deliver the rest of Israel into his hands.

David as a condition for the allegiance asked for Michal, his first wife, to be restored back to him. David sent a message to Ishbosheth asking for the return of Michal which Ishbosheth fulfilled. Michal had remarried by this time to a man from Paltiel the son of Laish, she was taken away from her new husband and returned to David.

Make People Feel Valued

David placed maximum value on all his assets, he recalled what it had cost him to marry Michal and he was not ready to lose that, though we are told that he already had about six other wives at this time.

Make every member of your team to feel valued, celebrate the least of them, the same way you would celebrate the most senior. As a popular Human Resource phrase goes 'it costs more to recruit than to retain'. There is a certain level of investment that has been made on every member of a team, be it in experience gained, training given, or just the mere fact that they understand how the wheel of the team works. They are therefore more valuable than any other like for like replacement. If they are being replaced by a more experienced person, then it would come at a higher cost.

Part of being an effective leader is to make people feel valuable; when you show people that they are an important part of the team or that you place considerable value on them, most likely than not, they will make better effort at a valuable contribution.

Do Not Be Wasteful

As the head of a household or church, do you have an inventory of all the assets you possess? Most of us have a rough estimated record of our most valuable assets – Cash at hand, in the bank,

Properties, Stocks, and Automobiles etc. We however do not have a record of the more basic things like the special occasion cutlery pieces or even our clothes. These basic items when all added together could be worth a small fortune, but we overlook them. If something has been acquired at a cost, then do not trivialise it; do not be wasteful as a leader.

Jesus asked the disciples to pick up the fragments from the multiplied five loaves of bread and two fish in John 6:12-13,

> *"So when they were filled, He said to His disciples, "Gather up the fragments that remain, so that nothing is lost." Therefore they gathered them up, and filled twelve baskets with the fragments of the five barley loaves which were left over by those who had eaten."*

Always gather up the fragments, no matter how much in abundance the item may be.

Jesus spoke in parables about the lost sheep and the lost coin to teach lessons on how valuable each soul is to God. Luke 15:3-10,

> *"What man of you, having a hundred sheep, if he loses one of them, does not leave*

the ninety-nine in the wilderness, and go after the one which is lost until he finds it? "And when he has found it, he lays it on his shoulders, rejoicing. "And when he comes home, he calls together his friends and neighbours, saying to them, 'Rejoice with me, for I have found my sheep which was lost!' "I say to you that likewise there will be more joy in heaven over one sinner who repents than over ninety-nine just persons who need no repentance. "Or what woman, having ten silver coins, if she loses one coin, does not light a lamp, sweep the house, and search carefully until she finds it? "And when she has found it, she calls her friends and neighbors together, saying, 'Rejoice with me, for I have found the piece which I lost! "Likewise, I say to you, there is joy in the presence of the angels of God over one sinner who repents."

The man with a hundred sheep could have allowed the one lost sheep to go away as he still had ninety-nine, why risk all over one? That is not the mentality of a great leader, each asset is of significant value.

CHAPTER 12

Do Not Be A Title Only In Name

"And when all the people came to persuade David to eat food while it was still day, David took an oath, saying, "God do so to me, and more also, if I taste bread or anything else till the sun goes down!" Now all the people took note of it, and it pleased them, since whatever the king did pleased all the people" (2 Samuel 3:35-36).

Not everybody in David's camp was pleased with Abner's defection to David, particularly Joab. Abner had killed Joab's brother in battle and he was seeking revenge. When he returned from one of his raids and was told that Abner had visited David earlier on, he was very displeased and told David that he was suspicious of Abner. After leaving David's presence, he sent messengers after Abner and requested for a private meeting . Abner did not suspect anything and agreed to turn back to meet with Joab. As the two men met, Joab had a concealed weapon on him with which he used to stab Abner to death. When David heard of Abner's death, he was again distraught and mourned for Abner, refusing to eat all day. The people in David's camp all mourned with David following his instructions. The people's loyalty to David was unwavering; they followed his instructions without questions because they loved David.

Gain Respect And Acceptability

David had widespread acceptance amongst the people he led. It was more than what he said or demanded but more about who he was.

A lot of leaders cling onto power selfishly because they know that it is the office they are holding that confers their acceptability. It is amazing that several leaders do not have any relevance immediately they are out of office; people only accepted them because of the office they held.

Several leaders have had erstwhile supporters turn against them at the slightest opportunity.

The people you are leading should respect you and not just your office, so that in or out of office, your level of influence and acceptability should not change. When people have a higher respect for your office over your person, it means you are not big enough to occupy that office. Some world leaders have actually elevated the office they hold to a higher degree of prominence by their personality whilst others have demeaned their office. There are some positions that did not have much importance attached to it till certain persons occupied that role and all of a sudden the office became a much-sought position.

A lot of children cannot wait to grow up and gain their independence as they only respected their parents because they were answerable to them. When the only influence you have over your children is the fact that you provide for their upkeep, then you are not fulfilling your role as a leader. If the children find an alternative for their welfare then you are no longer relevant to them.

Win Hearts

It is important that a leader has both character and charisma.

Renowned leaders in the world such as J.F. Kennedy had a lot of charisma that people overlooked their several indiscretions, whilst in office

Abraham Lincoln, Nelson Mandela, Obafemi Awolowo of Nigeria were leaders with character that today they are still reference points of what a leader should be

David had flaws in his character, but his charisma and sincerity could not be faulted.

When Absalom, David's son chose to revolt against him and David had to flee from Jerusalem, it was recorded that over six hundred men chose to go with David.

> *"Now a messenger came to David, saying, "The hearts of the men of Israel are with Absalom" So David said to all his servants who were with him at Jerusalem, "Arise, and let us flee, or we shall not escape from Absalom. Make haste to depart, lest he overtake us suddenly and bring disaster upon us, and strike the city with the edge of*

the sword." And the king's servants said to the king, "We are your servants, ready to do whatever my lord the king commands." Then all his servants passed before him; and all the Cherethites, all the Pelethites, and all the Gittites, six hundred men who had followed him from Gath, passed before the king" (2 Samuel 15:13-15, 18).

As David and his procession departed from Jerusalem, it is recorded,

"And all the country wept with a loud voice, and all the people crossed over. The king himself also crossed over the Brook Kidron, and all the people crossed over toward the way of the wilderness" (2 Samuel 15:23).

David had to send back several of the people who wanted to follow him on exile. These people were not following David because they stand to gain anything from him; there was no guarantee that he would return to his throne. They were ready to leave all behind and follow a true leader. They were doing this at great risks to their lives as Absalom would sooner have them all killed if his plan had worked out.

There are several instances when a leader is deposed and the whole country would burst out in jubilation.

I have heard the case of a leader of a corporate entity who was schemed out by supposedly trusted aides; he had granted a lot of favours to these aides and he expected their loyalty in return. Members of a team see beyond the bread crumbs that are handed out to them once in a while to what lies beneath the person holding the office (the real man).

CHAPTER 13

Be Consistent And Principled

"But David answered Rechab and Baanah his brother, the sons of Rimmon the Beerothite, and said to them, "As the LORD lives, who has redeemed my life from all adversity, "when someone told me, saying, 'Look, Saul is dead,' thinking to have brought good news, I arrested him and had him executed in Ziklag—the one who thought I would give him a reward for his news. "How much more, when wicked men have killed a righteous person in his own house on his bed? Therefore, shall I not now require his blood at your

> *hand and remove you from the earth?" So David commanded his young men, and they executed them, cut off their hands and feet, and hanged them by the pool in Hebron. But they took the head of Ishbosheth and buried it in the tomb of Abner in Hebron"* (2 Samuel 4:9-12).

When Ishbosheth learnt that Abner had been killed, he became distraught as Abner was his pillar and source of strength.

There were two men who were captains in his army who decided to gain favour with David by murdering Ishbosheth. They crept into the king's palace whilst he was asleep and stabbed him in the stomach thereby killing him. They were not satisfied with that and wanted to show David proof of what they had done, so they beheaded Ishbosheth and took his head along to show to David.

They escaped and travelled to meet with David at Hebron and showed him Ishbosheth's head and swore allegiance to David. They expected David to rejoice at the misfortune of Ishbosheth, who was the last piece of obstacle between himself and the throne.

However, if they had known David well enough, they would have known that David spared the life of Saul twice, they would have known that David had another man killed who came to him under the false pretence that he had killed Saul.

David's men who knew David's values would have stood by to see what David would do in this new instance. Would he treat this situation any different from the way he had acted before, it's been several years now and he was not yet king over Israel so would the attraction of having the obstacle in his part removed tempt him?

Have Personal Principles

David was consistent in his dealings with issues based on beliefs and principles. The reason why we are inconsistent at times in our dealings with people is because we do not have personal principles that guide our actions; we react to situations or issues based on emotions. Someone who is acting on principles will take some actions that will not be personally favourable.

A leader must have principles that are based on the right values, in order to ensure consistency of actions. These values would underpin decision-making.

David's values were based on a fear of God and that was the reason why he would not touch a reigning king of Israel nor accommodate anybody else that had violated these values.

When members of your team understand your value system, they will appreciate and respect them.

Live By Your Principles

A lot of fathers preach one thing to their children but practise something else. What you don't personally practise would not be respected by others.

In a democratic system, it is a lot harder to live by personal principles as there are so many different factions to please. Doing the right thing however is the difference between being a leader and being a great leader.

The Bible warns about not being a cheat, but also importantly about not having different standards,

> *"Diverse weights and diverse measures, they are both alike, an abomination to the LORD"* (Proverbs 20:10).

A leader cannot afford to be partial when dealing with people; different classes of people would require varying approaches to engagement but the same level of transparency, justice, equity etc. should be applied across.

Unfortunately for Pastors, the principles to live by are well documented and are public knowledge; there is therefore more scrutiny on their lives. These principles are based on grace and love and there is very little room for manoeuvre. Pastors should check their every actions and decisions whether it complies with these principles.

CHAPTER 14

Be Unassuming

"So David knew that the LORD had established him as king over Israel, and that He had exalted His kingdom for the sake of His people Israel" (2 Samuel 5:12).

In the fifth chapter of 2 Samuel, we see David becoming the King over the united Israelite nation. He began to consolidate his kingdom with conquests, especially that of the heavily fortified city of the Jebusites. David then established a stronghold for himself in Jerusalem and it was known as the City of David.

Focus On The Need Not Self

The Bible testified that David grew in influence, stature and prominence with God on his side. It was at the height of all these that David had a moment of introspection to understand that all that was happening was not about him.

It is very unusual for a leader to be able to see things differently at the height of his fame, with all the adulation and hero worship. History is replete with several leaders who have allowed success to get into their heads and who went on to declare themselves as gods because of their level of achievements.

God did not exalt the Kingdom for the sake of David, but for his people's sake. It is important that, as a leader, you identify the needs of the people you are leading and focus on those as your objectives rather than trying to achieve a personal objective. It would also be very wrong to try and use people you are leading to achieve an objective that is different from that which will bring collective good.

Leaders in the church are gifted according to their assignment and calling. They must not begin to see themselves as being on a different level from the congregation; living the life of a celebrity, hiring bodyguards, having all types of hangers on and praise singers. The only spiritual royalty in the church is The Lord Jesus and all the praise and adoration goes to Him. For everybody else, it is a privilege to have been called into His service. The level of success you will enjoy will be based on how you deal with the people that God has put you in charge of. There are times when your success will be dependent on how strong your congregation is, so you should also devote quality time to building up the capability of your people.

Be The Right Fit

In most instances where a leader is appointed, anointed or elected, the people doing the choosing do so, not just because the leader has got all the right qualities, but because they believe those qualities are the right fit with the need of the team at that point in time. So it is possible that a candidate might have very desirable qualities but that those qualities do not match what it will take to achieve the immediate or long term objectives of the people or organisation.

CHAPTER 15

Do Not Be Presumptuous

"Then the Philistines went up once again and deployed themselves in the Valley of Rephaim. Therefore David inquired of the LORD, and He said, "You shall not go up; circle around behind them, and come upon them in front of the mulberry trees" (2 Samuel 5:23).

When the Philistines heard that David had been crowned king over all of Israel, they gathered themselves for battle against the Israelites again.

David asked God for direction and backing for the battle against the Philistines and God gave him the go-ahead. David organised his army for battle and they assembled in a place called Baal Perazim where they defeated the Philistine army.

The Philistines were however not yet totally subdued and after some time, they once again gathered in the same valley of Rephaim for battle against the Israelite army.

It was the same Philistine army that he had defeated who gathered in exactly the same place where they had in the earlier battle. It was a no brainer to expect that David and his army would once again move out and rout the Philistines just as before.

David did not assume that he could use the same solution as he had used earlier for the same situation. David went back to God to make enquiries about the new battle and God gave him a completely different strategy to use. David did as God had instructed and he was able to defeat the Philistines and drive them back.

There are times when similar problems would necessitate a completely different approach to resolve it. No matter how similar a problem or situation looks, a leader should not be presumptuous that the same solution as applied in an earlier situation will always work. Every situation should be appraised on its merit; no matter what, there will be something different the second or third time around. It could be as simple as just the fact that there has been passage of time and with the rate of technological advancement and new discoveries, a different solution might be applicable.

CHAPTER 16

Learn From Previous Mistakes

"So they set the ark of God on a new cart, and brought it out of the house of Abinadab, which was on the hill; and Uzzah and Ahio, the sons of Abinadab, drove the new cart. So David would not move the ark of the LORD with him into the City of David; but David took it aside into the house of Obed-Edom the Gittite. Now it was told King David, saying, "The LORD has blessed the house of Obed-Edom and all that belongs to him, because of the ark of God." So David went and brought up the ark of God from the house of Obed-

Edom to the City of David with gladness. And so it was, when those bearing the ark of the LORD had gone six paces, that he sacrificed oxen and fatted sheep" (2 Samuel 6:3,10,12-13).

As David established himself as King over all of Israel and consolidated his kingdom through conquests, he decided to bring the ark of God to Jerusalem. The ark had all along been in the house of Abinadab.

In his preparation to move the ark of God, David got a new cart driven by two sons of Abinadab and pulled by oxen. The ark of God was placed on the cart and a procession of singers and instrumentalists went before the cart. As the procession moved along, they got to a place called Nachon's threshing floor and the oxen pulling the cart stumbled. Uzzah, one of the sons of Abinadab put his hands on the ark of God to try and steady it. This was however a mistake as God had commanded that only the priests were allowed to touch the ark. God was angry with Uzzah's mistake and he paid the ultimate penalty for his error with his life. Everybody in the procession was greatly terrified and David's fear of the Lord was increased that day. He halted the procession and directed that the ark could not be carried into Jerusalem any longer. The ark was then taken into the house of Obed-Edom and left there for the next three months.

There were laid down instructions by God on handling of the Ark of the Covenant which David had ignored during the first attempt to move the Ark.

> *"But thou shalt appoint the Levites over the tabernacle of testimony, and over all the vessels thereof, and over all things that belong to it: they shall bear the tabernacle, and all the vessels thereof; and they shall minister unto it, and shall encamp round about the tabernacle. And when the tabernacle setteth forward, the Levites shall take it down: and when the tabernacle is to be pitched, the Levites shall set it up: and the stranger that cometh nigh shall be put to death"* (Numbers 1:50–51).

"At that time the LORD separated the tribe of Levi, to bear the ark of the covenant of the LORD, to stand before the LORD to minister unto him, and to bless in his name, unto this day" (Deuteronomy 10:8).

As the time passed, the people noticed that the blessing of The Lord was upon the house of Obed-Edom as the household prospered. This was reported to David and he decided to once again move the ark into Jerusalem.

Review And Re-Strategise

This time around, David ensured that the tactics to move the ark was different; he got the Levites to carry the ark rather than putting it on a cart and had a steady supply of sacrifices ready as they moved along. The ark was then successfully carried into Jerusalem.

David did not repeat the same mistake he made during the first attempt to retrieve the ark. Just as he had not repeated the same victory tactics hoping for a similar result, he also did not repeat the same mistake hoping for a different result

A critical management practice is always to carry out periodic reviews:

- What are our goals/objectives?
- Where were we?
- Where are we now?
- What did we do right?

- What did we do wrong?

Turn Weaknesses Into Strengths

In performing a review of past actions or programmes, it is important that the weaknesses and strengths are clearly identified to understand what the underlying reasons for successes or failures were.

A great leader will utilise this information to bounce back from occasions of defeat and rally the team to use the setback as a stepping stone for greater achievements. The leader has to be able to motivate the team and rouse their spirit; it is normal that a setback or major defeat creates a psychological scar in the mind. The ability to put things behind and overcome adversities is a hallmark of champions and great leadership.

In a recent football match in England, in the Barclays Premier League, Arsenal played against Liverpool at Anfield (home of Liverpool FC) and having gone 2-1 up into the last minutes of the game, Liverpool came back to equalise and drew the game. In the same fixture in the previous season, Liverpool had won the game by 5 goals to 1. The Arsenal manager used the 5-1 loss of the previous visit to Anfield to explain that the Arsenal team were psychologically affected and could not play to their true potential. Some others might be of the view that it was an improvement to have come away with a 2-2 draw after having lost 5-1 previously. The job of a great leader would have been to use the 5-1 defeat as a motivational factor to bring out the best in the team instead of the defeat being a limiting factor.

CHAPTER 17

Give Honour

"Then Toi sent Joram his son unto king David, to salute him, and to bless him, because he had fought against Hadadezer, and smitten him: for Hadadezer had wars with Toi. And Joram brought with him vessels of silver, and vessels of gold, and vessels of brass: Which also king David did dedicate unto the LORD, with the silver and gold that he had dedicated of all nations which he subdued" (2 Samuel 8:11).

David, in all his successes and victories, still recognised that it was all due to The Lord's help. He therefore continued to honour The Lord to the best of his abilities. Wherever we may find ourselves in life, let us continue to honour those who facilitated our success or played a role in one way or the other.

No Role Is Supreme

In the different positions of leadership we may occupy, there is usually someone greater than us either directly or indirectly. There is the popular story of Steve Jobs being asked to step down from the same company that he co-founded. Presidents of nations have been impeached, company Directors have also been removed.

The only person without a superior is God and if that is not you, you have to come to the realisation that there are others who hold the reins to the very same power that you wield.

The ultimate honour should always be given to God

> *"But I would have you know, that the head of every man is Christ; and the head of the woman is the man; and the head of Christ is God"* (1 Corinthians 11:3).

Remember Your Supporters

Honour should also be given to our subordinates; the mighty men of valour who supported David were listed out as a sign of honour.

> *"These are the names of the mighty men whom David had: Josheb-Basshebethfn the Tachmonite, chief among the captains. He was called Adino the Eznite, because he had killed eight hundred men at one time. And after him was Eleazar the son of Dodo, the Ahohite, one of the three mighty men with David when they defied the Philistines who were gathered there for battle, and the men of Israel had retreated. He arose and attacked the Philistines until his hand was weary, and his hand stuck to the sword. The LORD brought about a great victory that day; and the people returned after him only to plunder. And after him was Shammah the son of Agee the Hararite. The Philistines had gathered together into a troop where there was a piece of ground full of lentils. So the people fled from the Philistines. But he stationed himself in the middle of the field, defended it, and killed the Philistines. So the*

LORD brought about a great victory. Then three of the thirty chief men went down at harvest time and came to David at the cave of Adullam. And the troop of Philistines encamped in the Valley of Rephaim. Now Abishai the brother of Joab, the son of Zeruiah, was chief of another three. He lifted his spear against three hundred men, killed them, and won a name among these three. Was he not the most honored of three? Therefore he became their captain. However, he did not attain to the first three. Benaiah was the son of Jehoiada, the son of a valiant man from Kabzeel, who had done many deeds. He had killed two lion-like heroes of Moab. He also had gone down and killed a lion in the midst of a pit on a snowy day. And he killed an Egyptian, a spectacular man. The Egyptian had a spear in his hand; so he went down to him with a staff, wrested the spear out of the Egyptian's hand, and killed him with his own spear. These things Benaiah the son of Jehoiada did, and won a name among three mighty men. He was more honored than the thirty, but he did not attain to the first three. And David appointed him over his guard. Asahel the brother of Joab was one of the thirty; Elhanan the son of Dodo of Bethlehem, Shammah the Harodite, Elika the Harodite, Helez the Paltite, Ira the son of Ikkesh the Tekoite, Abiezer the Anathothite, Mebunnai the Hushathite, Zalmon the Ahohite, Maharai the Netophathite, Heleb the son of Baanah (the Netophathite), Ittai the son of Ribai from Gibeah of the children of Benjamin, Benaiah a Pirathonite, Hiddai from the brooks of Gaash, Abi-Albon the Arbathite, Azmaveth the Barhumite, Eliahba the Shaalbonite (of the sons of Jashen), Jonathan Shammah the Hararite, Ahiam the son of Sharar the Hararite, Eliphelet the son of Ahasbai, the son of the Maachathite, Eliam the son of Ahithophel the Gilonite, Hezrai the Carmelite, Paarai the Arbite, Igal the son of Nathan of Zobah, Bani the Gadite Zelek the Ammonite, Naharai the Beerothite (armorbearer of Joab the son of Zeruiah) Ira the Ithrite, Gareb the Ithrite, and Uriah the Hittite: thirty-seven in all" (2 Samuel 23:8-13, 18-31).

Almost a whole chapter is devoted to recording the deeds of the mighty men who supported David; this shows that it was never disguised to look like a one man show. David must have ensured that his men were duly recognized and honoured.

Be Wary Of Changes In Circumstances

There are situations and circumstances that also combine to influence the emergence or demotion of some leaders e.g. the assassination of JFK led to Lyndon B Johnson becoming the 36th President of the United States, the abdication of the throne by King Edward VIII led to his succession by the then Duke of York. King Constantine II of Greece was deposed as king with the abolition of the monarchy in 1973. Julius Caesar was assassinated through a conspiracy by many Roman senators just after being declared dictator perpetuo by the senate.

Instances such as these should keep leaders humble, that tomorrow is not always as secure as it appears to be. Today's deputy could become tomorrow's leader; the high handedness that they were subjected to under today's leadership may be repaid many times over.

CHAPTER 18

Identify With Others

"Therefore Hanun took David's servants, shaved off half of their beards, cut off their garments in the middle, at their buttocks, and sent them away. When they told David, he sent to meet them, because the men were greatly ashamed. And the king said, "Wait at Jericho until your beards have grown, and then return" 2 Samuel 10:4-5).

One of David's allies, the king of Ammon died and his son Hanun was crowned as king in his stead. David wanted to commiserate with Hanun over the death of his father and to congratulate him on his ascension to the throne, so he sent over a delegation.

The advisors of the new king Hanun were however suspicious of David's actions and misinterpreted his intentions. They told the king that David had sent the men as spies in order to eventually overthrow the new king and take over Ammon.

The new king, in order to demonstrate his authority and might, commanded that the men who had been sent from David should be utterly humiliated as a message to David.

Have Respect For People's Values

David knew the symbolic significance of the beards to the men and he was concerned enough with their honour.

It is forbidden, under the Levitical law, for a man to shave the 'side-growth' of his beard (Leveticus 19:27 & 21:5). Furthermore, shaving was considered a pagan practice and consequently was not acceptable. The beard was also a means by which men and women could be distinguished, it was a manly symbol. A man that is clean shaven was considered effeminate and despised. The men that had been so humiliated by Hanun were therefore too shamed to return back to Jerusalem.

David was concerned enough about the feelings of his servants and covered their shame by asking them to stay at Jericho till their beards regrow. Even the lowliest associate deserves every form of courtesy.

How well do you know the individual members of your team? You should know the various things they hold dear, their spouses, family members, beliefs, passions, etc. If you place the right value on your team members, then you will respect the things they also value.

These things might seem trivial, but they are valuable loyalty currencies. Remembering the birthdays of your team members or even their anniversaries will endear you to your team members.

Take Special Interest In Those Close To You

It's so easy to overlook the feelings or welfare of close servants because they are taken for granted. Sometimes, it is the very loyal servant or member of staff that is taken for granted; these are the ones that never complain and always seem to agree with you as the leader. The leader often assumes that they are satisfied and doesn't really bother to know their true feelings. Loyalty should be rewarded and thereby encouraged, special privileges should be granted, but more importantly such servants or followers should have a special place in the heart of the leader.

Massive crowd followed Jesus during His earthly ministry; a separate group from the crowd was the twelve disciples. Among the twelve disciples, Peter, James and John enjoyed a closer relationship. In his epistle, John referred to himself in different instances as the disciple whom Jesus loved (John 20:2, John 21:7, John 21:20). It is therefore not surprising that when Jesus was on the cross, He entrusted the care of Mary (mother of Jesus) to the care of this same disciple (John 19:21). Most leaders would not be able to do this because they hardly know their loyal followers apart from the fact that they are doing a very good job. A leader should know as much as possible about the loyal followers, even up to the point of prying, let the follower be the one to draw the line on how far you can go.

People link your servants to you as a leader e.g. the driver of the MD, secretary to the CEO, Chief of staff to the Governor etc. Your servants are therefore an extension of yourself in a way; they project you and your values. You cannot therefore be a person of integrity and have people with a questionable personality representing you, even as a driver. You need to know what values your followers or servants hold dear, what they believe in and things that are most important to them. A leader also needs to be able to instil his values and image into his followers. The people you employ or who make up the bulk of your followers define how you are perceived by people. If all your employees or followers come from a particular ethnic background, then you are creating the impression of being intolerant, non-accommodating, and biased or not having the ability to reach across to a wider pool.

Bond With Your People

Jesus visiting Peter's house and healing his wife's mother (Matthew 8:14-15) demonstrated that Jesus identified with His disciples on a personal basis. Jesus knew Peter's house and was able to drop in for a visit; Jesus did not feel too high and mighty as the son of God to be found visiting the house of an ordinary disciple. Jesus could have used the excuse that Peter is with Him always and all days and there was no need to go visiting, with all the work that needed to be accomplished.

Recall good and bad times with your team members to help the bonding process; the failures are as important as the victories. The memories of the things you have been through together create a special connection that cannot be easily forgotten. It helps the relationship between leader and followers to know that you have both stood together through the rough patches as well as the times of celebration. The followers will feel more confident that they can count on their leader to stand by them and with them when things are rough.

Attending your children's school productions, games or performances lets them know that they are important to you. Any child will draw inspiration just by looking into the crowd or audience and seeing the parents cheering. As a parent you should know your children better than their teachers; you should know their interests, likes and dislikes. You should know what choices they will make when given certain opportunities. This can only come through spending time with them and active engagement with them.

CHAPTER 19

Get The Right Support Structure

"And Joab the son of Zeruiah was over the host; and Jehoshaphat the son of Ahilud was recorder; And Zadok the son of Ahitub, and Ahimelech the son of Abiathar, were the priests; and Seraia was the scribe; And Benaiah the son of Jehoiada was over both the Cherethites and the Pelethites; and David's sons were chief rulers" (2 Samuel 8:16-18).

David had officials in place who were competent to fulfil the roles they had been assigned.

He did not place people in positions based on sentiments or relationships.

A great leader builds a great team; the team does not have to consist of superstars, what is important is that the sum of the parts be greater than the individual parts.

Learn To Delegate

Too many leaders try to do it all alone, they handle the finances, the administration, the technical and every other thing that falls in between.

In Exodus 18:13-23, we read the following account transpiring between Moses and his father-in-law,

> *"And so it was, on the next day, that Moses sat to judge the people; and the people stood before Moses from morning until evening. So when Moses' father-in-law saw all that he did for the people, he said, "What is this thing that you are doing for the people? Why do you alone sit, and all the people stand before you from morning until evening?" And Moses said to his father-in-law, "Because the people come to me to inquire of God. "When they have a*

difficulty, they come to me, and I judge between one and another; and I make known the statutes of God and His laws." So Moses' father-in-law said to him, "The thing that you do is not good. "Both you and these people who are with you will surely wear yourselves out. For this thing is too much for you; you are not able to perform it by yourself. "Listen now to my voice; I will give you counsel, and God will be with you: Stand before God for the people, so that you may bring the difficulties to God. "And you shall teach them the statutes and the laws, and show them the way in which they must walk and the work they must do. "Moreover you shall select from all the people able men, such as fear God, men of truth, hating covetousness; and place such over them to be rulers of thousands, rulers of hundreds, rulers of fifties, and rulers of tens. "And let them judge the people at all times. Then it will be that every great matter they shall bring to you, but every small matter they themselves shall judge. So it will be easier for you, for they will bear the burden with you. "If you do this thing, and

God so commands you, then you will be able to endure, and all this people will also go to their place in peace."

What we see here is Moses being taught the rudiments of delegation by his father-in-law, a Gentile priest. Moses would have worn himself out by ministering to the entire Israelite camp from morning to evening, as he was doing. When would he have had time for himself or even to attend to things of more spiritual or strategic significance?

Empower Your Subordinates

A lot of leaders are scared to let go of authority or responsibilities either through insecurity of their position or simply because they want to be in charge of everything. Some leaders go ahead and appoint subordinates into positions of accountability but still do not relinquish such responsibilities, thereby making such appointees redundant. A leader should not appoint people into positions and still go ahead to be performing the duties that have been assigned to others to perform. It weakens the assigned authority and also shows the leader as making the wrong choices of putting the wrong people into authority. The leader should also ensure that people being led respect the lines of hierarchy; issues should first be discussed with the sectional heads where there is one in place and only should be brought to the leader when it cannot be addressed at the sectional head's level. The leader is kept informed and updated regularly by the sectional heads of the various issues within their areas of responsibility. It is the prerogative of the leader to ensure that he has complete oversight of the different situations within the team.

Getting the right support structure is not a sign of incompetence and should also not be treated as abandoning responsibility. The ultimate responsibility still lies with the leader and whatever decision is taken by the people appointed into positions is backed and binding on the leader.

Choose A Team That Complements

A leader should not accuse his appointees, leadership team or officers as being incompetent because he has the right to determine those working with him. Choosing the right set of people is important; if the leader is the type that likes to micro-manage then it would be wrong to appoint people who like to work independently of micro supervision. Get people whom you can work with that will complement your style of leadership.

Assembling a team that is not only functional but effective is a great leadership skill; it involves selecting people who not only are a complement to the leader but who also work well together as a team. At times, they might not be the finished article but they have the potential that can be nurtured. The leader has to be able to motivate and develop his team, see character form in them and make them perform above expectations. Too many leaders do not have the patience to build a team; they expect to just assemble a group of superstars and for every other thing to fall into place.

The support group or team should be a reflection of the leader, not clones of the leader. By being a reflection, it means they understand and accept the vision of the leader and they are ready to run with it. It is the responsibility of the leader to also spend time with the leadership team to know them and be known by them. It will not always be achievable at official meetings, but spending quality time together informally to get team dynamics right.

In the family setting, having the right support structure starts with seeing your spouse as a complement. Don't overlook the valuable contribution that your spouse brings; understand her strength, encourage her and work with her.

CHAPTER 20

Manage Setbacks

"Now therefore the sword shall never depart from thine house; because thou hast despised me, and hast taken the wife of Uriah the Hittite to be thy wife. And he said, While the child was yet alive, I fasted and wept: for I said, who can tell whether GOD will be gracious to me, that the child may live? But now he is dead, wherefore should I fast? Can I bring him back again? I shall go to him, but he shall not return to me" (2 Samuel 12:10; 2 Samuel 12:22-23).

One of the biggest misdeeds that David committed in his lifetime was his affair with Bathsheba, the wife of Uriah.

David had taken a liking to Bathsheba whilst her husband was at the war front; he invited her over to the palace and slept with her. Bathsheba became pregnant and David tried to cover up the affair. He recalled Uriah from the war front and asked him to go and spend the night at home. Uriah did not comply with the orders due to his sense of loyalty to the war cause. When David saw that he could not achieve his ploy through this deceit, he had Uriah set up on the battlefield and got him killed. David thereafter went ahead to marry the already pregnant Bathsheba.

God sent a message to David through the Prophet Nathan and the consequences of his actions were to be both immediate and long term. The immediate consequence was that the child conceived through the adulterous act would die.

The child became ill and all through the time he was ill, David fasted and prayed for the child that he would live. The child however did not survive the illness. After his death, David's servants were afraid to let him know that the child had died. They reasoned that if David had refused to eat whilst the child was ill then how would he handle the death of the child. To their utmost surprise when David got to know that the child was dead, he brightened up; freshened up and had his meal.

Learn To Move On

There are many mistakes that cannot be undone and it is of no use crying over spilt milk. The concept is to review the mistake, take the lessons learned, move on and don't repeat the same mistake again.

A great leader should be able to manage situations that are setbacks. Put ugly situations behind your back and move on to the next objective. It is about understanding that every journey is a combination of valleys and hills; there will be times of victories but also those times of setbacks.

Be Prepared For Challenges

In car designs, emphasis is laid on ensuring that the car delivers as smooth a journey as possible; so you have the shock absorbers, bushings and tyre specifications. The quality of a car is expressed by minimising the various imperfections on the road to ensure the occupant does not feel them. A leader should not only have the capacity within him to handle the rough times but should also have built in those shock absorbers into the team to overcome the rough terrain. There should be contingency plans in place to kick in when the setbacks occur. Every plan, budget or proposal should have proactive 'what if' scenarios built in. Agreed that you cannot envisage every type of setback, but being able to react appropriately is also determined by how well prepared the leader is.

In Luke 14:28-33, Jesus taught about the preparedness of becoming a disciple; part of which involves planning for various scenarios. It is about being well prepared for different eventualities and knowing that it will not always go your way.

> *"For which of you, intending to build a tower, does not sit down first and count the cost, whether he has enough to finish it — "lest, after he has laid the foundation, and is not able to finish, all who see it begin to mock him, "saying, 'This man began to build and was not able to finish.' "Or what king, going to make war against another king, does not sit down first and consider whether he is able with ten thousand to meet him who comes against him with*

> *twenty thousand? "Or else, while the other is still a great way off, he sends a delegation and asks conditions of peace. "So likewise, whoever of you does not forsake all that he has cannot be My disciple."*

This might seem contrary to the faith message; you might ask: why should a Christian plan for defeat, when Christ has promised us victory in all situations?

A Christian leader should know that one other thing that Jesus promised is that attacks would come; being well prepared for those attacks will prevent them from turning into defeats. At times, real setbacks do occur and that is when the inner strength and capacity is required to turn these moments around.

Tackle, Rather Than Avoid The Issue

> *"And they returned to Joshua and said to him, "Do not let all the people go up, but let about two or three thousand men go up and attack Ai. Do not weary all the people there, for the people of Ai are few." So about three thousand men went up there from the people, but they fled before the*

men of Ai. And the men of Ai struck down about thirty-six men, for they chased them from before the gate as far as Shebarim, and struck them down on the descent; therefore the hearts of the people melted and became like water. Then Joshua tore his clothes, and fell to the earth on his face before the ark of the LORD until evening, he and the elders of Israel; and they put dust on their heads. And Joshua said, "Alas, Lord GOD, why have You brought this people over the Jordan at all— to deliver us into the hand of the Amorites, to destroy us? Oh, that we had been content, and dwelt on the other side of the Jordan! "O Lord, what shall I say when Israel turns its back before its enemies? "For the Canaanites and all the inhabitants of the land will hear it, and surround us, and cut off our name from the earth. Then what will You do for Your great name?" So the LORD said to Joshua: "Get up! Why do you lie thus on your face?" (Joshua 7:3-10).

In the account above, the Israelites were supposed to have a routine battle against the people of Ai, but the outcome was a rout for the Israelites.

Their confidence was quickly replaced with shame and fear.

Joshua knew something had gone wrong and he gathered the elders together that they should seek the face of The Lord. The answer from The Lord was a sharp rebuke, not only for the sin of Israel but also to Joshua; Joshua had not spoken as a leader but was grovelling in front of the ark. He magnified the defeat to mean that The Lord had abandoned them and had handed them over to the mercy of their enemies. As a leader, he needed to have seen the defeat as an aberration and an unwelcomed development.

Thankfully, he had the grace upon him to go before The Lord and not to have given up in despair. The Lord then gave him instruction on what to do, as the defeat was as a result of transgression against expressly given instructions by one of the families in the camp of the Israelites.

KING DAVID - MASTER Class

CHAPTER 21

Plan For Posterity

"So Nathan spoke to Bathsheba the mother of Solomon, saying, "Have you not heard that Adonijah the son of Haggith has become King, and David our Lord does not know it? Come, please, let me now give you advice, that you may save your own life and the life of your son Solomon. Go immediately to King David and say to him, 'Did you not, my lord, O King, swear to your maidservant, saying, "Assuredly your son Solomon shall reign after me, and he shall sit on my throne"? Why then has Adonijah become king? And as for you, my lord, O king, the eyes of all Israel are on

you, that you should tell them who will sit on the throne of my lord the king after him. Otherwise it will happen, when my lord the king rests with his fathers, that I and my son Solomon will be counted as offenders" (1 Kings 1:11-13; 1 Kings 1:20-21).

The time came when David was now too old to effectively rule over his kingdom; he spent all his time in his chambers in the palace and his servants looked after him. The next in line to the throne was his son Adonijah; Absalom's younger brother. He had the physical attributes to be admired and he also played his cards well by enlisting Joab, the army general to his side. He proclaimed himself as King and got the priest Abiathar to perform the coronation ceremony.

The staunch loyalists to David however were not a part of the ploy as they knew that David wanted another one of his sons to succeed him as king. David had promised Bathsheba that his son Solomon would be king after him.

Groom A Successor

It is not recorded anywhere else in the Bible of any of the other kings choosing a successor. David did not follow the tradition of the succession to the throne, being by birth right. He must have had strong reasons as to why he did not want Adonijah to be king after him. From the actions of Adonijah in installing himself as the next king it can be deduced that he would have been the wrong choice for Israel. He represented what that is wrong with leadership by being self-centred, egoistical, conniving and divisive.

Solomon, on the other hand, led Israel through a forty year period of peaceful and prosperous reign; he strengthened the kingdom through diplomacy and by building strong alliances. His wisdom is unparalleled as recorded in the book of Proverbs and the splendour of his kingdom drew admirers from all over the world.

Israel would have missed this if David had not groomed and chosen his successor.

Prepare Him For Success

Leaders must plan for the success of the team after they must have exited the scene. A great leader is that person who ensures that his successor exceeds his own achievements. David was told by God that he would not be able to build the temple but that his son who would reign after him would be the one to build the temple for God. David did not go into a jealous fit as he wasn't being allowed to fulfil one of his greatest dreams that would have further cemented his name into the history of the nation Israel. David started to prepare all the materials that his son would require to put up one of the greatest edifice in the entire nation.

> *"Then David gave his son Solomon the plans for the vestibule, its houses, its treasuries, its upper chambers, its inner chambers, and the place of the mercy seat; and the plans for all that he had by the Spirit, of the courts of the house of the LORD, of all the chambers all around, of the treasuries of the house of God, and of the treasuries for the dedicated things; also for the division of the priests and the Levites, for all the work of the service of the house of the LORD, and for all the articles of service in the house of the LORD. He gave gold by weight for things of gold, for all articles used in every kind of service; also silver for all articles of silver by weight, for all articles used in every kind of service; the weight for the lampstands of gold, and their lamps of gold, by weight for each lampstand and its lamps; for the*

lampstands of silver by weight, for the lampstand and its lamps, according to the use of each lampstand. And by weight he gave gold for the tables of the showbread, for each table, and silver for the tables of silver; also pure gold for the forks, the basins, the pitchers of pure gold, and the golden bowls—he gave gold by weight for every bowl; and for the silver bowls, silver by weight for every bowl; and refined gold by weight for the altar of incense, and for the construction of the chariot, that is, the gold cherubim that spread their wings and overshadowed the ark of the covenant of the LORD" (1 Chronicles 28:11-18).

It is often said that true greatness is the ability to make others great.

Ensure Sustained Welfare

A truly great leader would ensure not only the continued success of the team after his exit but also the prosperity of the team. One of the fears of Bathsheba was that if Solomon did not become king as had been promised by David, the next king would see Solomon as a threat and would kill him, as well as her. You cannot be counted to be a great leader if you are not planning for posterity, for the wellbeing of those who would come after you. The government of Norway is reported to be investing the oil wealth of the nation to ensure that the future generations would not lack.

Joseph's counsel to Pharaoh after interpreting the dream of seven years of prosperity to be followed by seven years of famine, was that they should store up grains for the coming years of famine.

> *"Now therefore, let Pharaoh select a discerning and wise man, and set him over the land of Egypt. "Let Pharaoh do this, and let him appoint officers over the land, to collect one-fifth of the produce of the land of Egypt in the seven plentiful years. "And let them gather all the food of those good years that are coming, and store up grain under the authority of Pharaoh, and let them keep food in the cities. "Then that food shall be as a reserve for the land for the seven years of famine which shall be in the land of Egypt that the land may not perish during the famine"* (Genesis 41:33–36).

Many so-called leaders are eating away the future of their country whilst others are mortgaging the future for temporary gains.

A father must have a will in place that ensures that his family would not lack nor suffer after his demise.

Don't Leave A Vacuum

Pastors should have a recognised and respected No. 2 in place that would be able to carry on in their absence. I do recognise that most times a call to ministry can be specific to an individual e.g. Paul wrote to the Galatian church that the gospel for the uncircumcised was committed to him as the gospel for the circumcised was to Peter (Galatians 2:7). Paul did not start to run a solo ministry; he had several travel companions like Titus, Timothy, Luke, etc. In various instances, he asked Timothy to go and visit on his behalf some of the churches they had planted (1 Corinthians 4:17, Acts 19:22, 1 Thessalonians 3:2). The gospel to the uncircumcised did not die along with Paul nor did the strength of the message diminish in potency after his death. Ministries should not dwindle and fade away after the exit of the Pastor. Having a designated assistant in place in the ministry means the church recognises such a person as having the Pastor's authority to act when the Pastor is not around. It also means that the Pastor relinquishes his authority when he is travelling, there should not be a vacuum in the ministry. When a Pastor has to travel, it is important that there is someone authorized to act in his absence and the person must be duly acknowledged and recognised by the congregation rather than having a situation of church attendance dwindling because the Pastor is not around. Pastors should not be pastoring from some remote location and having every matter referred to them. If there is nobody in place competent enough to act in the place of the Pastor, then it is a challenge to the Pastor to groom someone to take up the position. Moses groomed Joshua, Elijah groomed Elisha, Paul groomed Timothy; and in all these instances, we see a smooth transition and transfer of authority.

CHAPTER 22

Fulfil Your Role

"And David reigned over all Israel; and David executed judgment and justice unto all his people" (2 Samuel 8:15).

"Now these are the last words of David.
Thus says David the son of Jesse;
Thus says the man raised up on high,
The anointed of the God of Jacob,
And the sweet psalmist of Israel:
"The Spirit of the LORD spoke by me,
And His word was on my tongue.

The God of Israel said,

The Rock of Israel spoke to me:

'He who rules over men must be just,

Ruling in the fear of God.

And he shall be like the light of the morning when the sun rises,

A morning without clouds,

Like the tender grass springing out of the earth,

By clear shining after rain" (2 Samuel 23:1-4).

In conclusion, after all that has been said and attributed to David, he had a testimony of his own experience and performance as a king; on his death bed he had a reminiscence based on what The Lord had told him.

Be Just

He said, "he who rules over men must be just". In the context in which David wrote, being just does not only refer to the execution of justice as a leader but also to the character of the leader.

The execution of justice involves treating others fairly, based on moral, philosophical, societal values or religious code. David qualified his sense of justice by continuing to say "ruling in the fear of God". He lived by this code and did not go about perverting the course of Justice.

David did the exact job he was called to do. A lot of people go through the motions of their jobs but do not achieve the purpose of the job. Knowing your job description and the immediate deliverables of the role is very paramount.

A just leader would not abuse his office or the privileges of that office; greed, corruption, avarice, misappropriation, recklessness etc. are not attributes of a good leader. Ruling in the fear of God means that that leader should be accountable to a higher authority.

An elected leader must be accountable to the people he is leading. A leader and the people being led should be subject and accountable to an agreed set of codified principles or a set of laws, like the leaders of most nations are subject to the laws of the land and the constitution. The leader should always be ready to be challenged, based on the laws the leader and the led have all agreed to follow.

If you have been elected to be the leader of a nation, be fair and equitable to all. Do not become a sectional leader; do not favour a group over another.

Leaders in corporate environments should also not be partial to one department over another. They may be the goose laying the golden egg, but there shouldn't be different sets of rules

Be Unbiased

David further went on to say "And he shall be like the light of the morning when the sun rises"

The light of the morning is bright and shines on all, regardless of who they are, so far as you are under the sky. A great leader must be impartial, not discriminating against people because they do not fit his self-styled standards. People are treated equally and with dignity and they are confident of always being treated fairly.

The light of the morning also signals the passing away of darkness and exposure of evils of the night. A great leader will not be associated with or cover up for workers of iniquity and corruption. It is not also about turning the blind eye to evil practice, but the leader actively works to expose such. Light and darkness cannot co-exist, so it should not be possible for shady characters to thrive and be comfortable in the team of such a leader.

Be Transparent

The leader should be "like the morning without clouds". This means, the leader is transparent for all to see, there are no nasty surprises. There is no unpredictability – will he or won't he. A morning with clouds puts a damp to the day, people are expecting the unwanted rain, but do not know when it will pour.

Be Pleasant

He is like the tender grass springing out of the earth – It is not a thorny growth that is unpleasant, dangerous and avoided. A great leader is tender in his dealings with people; he seeks peace and the wellbeing of the team.

www.ingramcontent.com/pod-product-compliance
Lightning Source LLC
Chambersburg PA
CBHW061947070426
42450CB00007BA/1078